Management
Moment
by Moment

Thoughts that help you to be responsible for yourself,
manage yourself and take control of your life

W0006388

J.P. Vaswani

Gita Publishing House
Pune, (India).
www.dadavaswanisbooks.org

Management
Moment
by Moment

Thoughts that help you to be responsible for yourself,
manage yourself and take control of your life

J.P. Vaswani

Gita Publishing House
Pune, (India).
www.dadavaswanisbooks.org

Published by:
Gita Publishing House
Sadhu Vaswani Mission,
10, Sadhu Vaswani Path,
Pune – 411 001, (India).
gph@sadhuvaswani.org

Third Edition

ISBN : 978-93-80743-03-5

Printed by:
Mehta Offset Pvt. Ltd.
Mehta House,
A-16, Naraina Industrial Area II,
New Delhi – 110 028, (India).
info@mehtaoffset.com

CONTENTS

The world today is full of tension. Wherever I go, I find people are tense and nervous. Stress and tension are more common in their incidence than the common cold.

Today hospitals are full of patients who suffer from diseases due to stress. Stress is the cause of a number of physical ailments. Stress keeps on accumulating in the minds of the people until, one day, it manifests itself in the form of one ailment or the other.

J.P. Vaswani

STRESS MANAGEMENT

Car drivers are so rash today. All drivers seem to be in a dreadful hurry to get somewhere - for the seed of rashness is in all of us. Traffic signals are meant to control this rashness and allow people to drive safely, smoothly across intersections. Alas, many of us have forgotten what signals are meant for. The Red says Stop; the Green says Go; and Amber tells us to Wait.

They asked a little boy if he knew what the lights in the traffic signals stood for. "Sure," he replied, "I've seen my daddy drive past so many signals. Red means stop; Green means go and Amber means speed up!"

WHAT IS STRESS?

- Stress has never been as commonplace as it is today! It is a bug that eats its way into the life of 8 out of every 10 people in the workforce.

- "Stress" originates from a French word which means constriction or delimitation. True it is that stress squeezes the life force in us.

- Stress has been known to have a snowballing effect. It keeps accumulating unless tackled or treated effectively.

- Stress also possesses a boomerang quality. It begins with the workplace, then affects the family front. It reverts back hitting work performance.

- Stress is subjective. What may cause extreme panic to one person may be just a cake-walk to the other.

- A certain amount of stress is called "necessary stress" which acts as a motivating force to achieve goals. For e.g. the stress involved in trying to win a tennis match.

FACT FILE

"Problem" is derived from the Latin word *Pro Balo* which means deliberately thrown in our way

CAUSES OF STRESS

- Frantic pace of modern lifestyle

- Desire to accomplish more than what one is normally capable of

- Competitive environment, compelling survival and success of the fittest

- Dissatisfaction due to non fulfillment of high expectations

- Resistance to people and situations creates inner unrest which when held in the long term aggravates into stress

- Exhaustion and fatigue add to more stress

- Extremely high demands and wants, excessive consumerism

- Problems which overwhelm people

- Lack of inner connection to one's true self, one's true nature

EFFECTS OF STRESS ON THE BODY

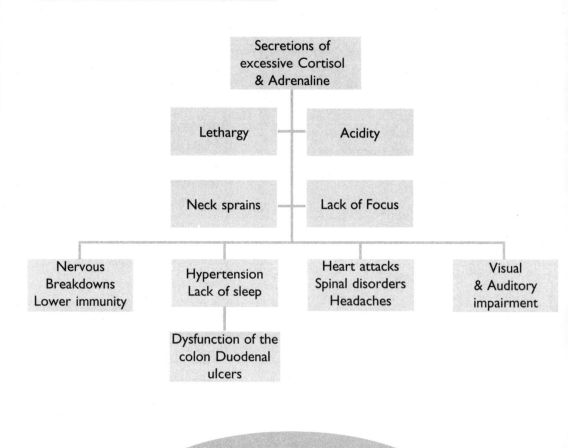

Medical researchers say that 90% diseases are stress related.

STRESS BUSTERS TO ERADICATE STRESS FROM THE HUMAN PSYCHE

Stress Buster No. 1

Revamp your attitude to a positive one

The workplace becomes akin to a jungle when situations and people get out of hand but our attitude can always be within our control and it can be a positive one.

Following are the steps to cultivate a positive attitude:

- Set aside time everyday to replenish your mind with positively charged thoughts.

- Whenever you feel you are gripped by negativity, fall back on some dynamic and inspiring thought from any scripture that appeals to you.

Inspiration

Unhappy and dejected, the amateur writer gave up hope of finding a publisher to print his work. In a moment of madness he threw his draft into the dustbin. Finding the abandoned manuscript in the basket, his wife picked it up and placed it before him, "My dear Norman, you cannot give up! Your work will get noticed and will surely be appreciated."

The author was Norman Vincent Peale and ironically the book was "The Power of Positive Thinking" which turned out to be an inspirational, best seller.

Stress Buster No. 2

Work in the consciousness of the present moment

When challenges stare at us, we are so overwhelmed by their sheer impact that we analyze its past and predict its effects on the future. It is important that we deal with the problem in the present moment consciousness. This helps to tackle the problem in a practical way.

Most of our lives are wasted either feeling guilty about the past or worrying about the future. Trying to be in another time zone whilst physically being present in the now is a big *stressor.*

---

1 "Attitudes are more important than facts."

-Karl Menninger

Schedule your activities in "day-tight compartments", which means to plan reasonably achievable goals within the framework of the day. Then completely focus only on those targets without thinking about jobs that are not planned for that day.

Inspiration

Live in the present moment

■ A simpleton was walking along the street when he was lost in deep thought. He was thinking about how he had escaped from a fire just a day earlier. So lost was he in thought that he began visualising the scene as he stopped on the street. He frantically waved his hands to and fro. People laughed at his predicament but no one realised that they too live either in the past or the future.

Watching this a *fakir* approached him with a ring. It had an inscription which said, "Welcome to the Now". The *fakir* kept repeating it again and again. "Welcome to the Now".

We all need to program our minds every time we slip away from the present, "Welcome to the Now".

An Attitude of Gratitude...

■ We can complain about our health problems or thank God that we are still able-bodied.

■ We can complain about lack or thank God that we have much more than the underprivileged.

■ We can complain about our jobs or thank God that we are not jobless.

■ We can complain about pollution, or begin planting trees.

■ We can complain about the flaws of a relative or a friend or thank God that we are not lonely.

Stress Buster No. 3

Try praise and appreciation, for a change...

- Use praise generously and sincerely

- Thank colleagues and subordinates for every little thing they do. There is no better motivator.

- Maintain a gratitude journal. Each day allot time to write a list of all the blessings and bounties that you have been taking for granted.

- Once you have developed a habit of being grateful, your focus will always be on the positive, thereby activating the law of attraction to fill your world with joy and plenty.

Inspiration

Some people work and become
  wealthy.
Others do the same and remain
  poor.
Marriage fills one with energy,
Another it drains.
Don't trust ways, they change.
Always add the gratitude-clause
to any sentence, *if God Wills*
Then go ahead...

Stress Buster No. 4

Streamline your Life

- Simplify and streamline everything from the workplace to the home front.

- At the workplace, delegate well, communicate efficiently, and use time management!

- Unclutter your mind as well as the space around you.

- Organise your work load to make it simple. Organise chores and errands at home on a priority basis. All this, once done in a systematic way, will reduce stress.

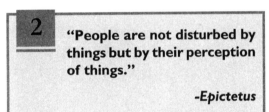

2 "People are not disturbed by things but by their perception of things."

-Epictetus

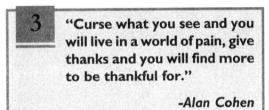

3 "Curse what you see and you will live in a world of pain, give thanks and you will find more to be thankful for."

-Alan Cohen

THREE-FOLD FORMULA FOR STRESS MANAGEMENT

Firstly, we must be careful to see that we always have a positive attitude towards life. By positive attitude, I do not mean that life does not have a negative side. Life does have a negative, a dark side. Life is full of difficulties and dangers, trials and tribulations. But the man with the positive approach refuses to dwell on the negative side of life. Surrounded by the most adverse conditions, he will look for a place to stand on. Conditions all around him may be frustrating, but he will not give up. He will continue to expect the best results and this is an inviolable law of life. What you expect persistently, comes rushing to you. For you only draw to yourselves, that which you think of all the time. Your thoughts are magnets. Through your thoughts, you draw to yourselves conditions and circumstances of which you keep on thinking all the time.

Always have a constructive, positive approach towards life. There is a picture I saw many years ago. It was a

picture of two buckets, each half filled with water. Outside one bucket, there was a face with a frown and underneath were written the words, "Of what use is it to be half empty all the time?" Outside the other bucket, there was a face with a smile and underneath were the words, "I feel grateful to God that I am at least half full all the time." The two buckets symbolise the negative and positive attitudes towards life. The man with the negative attitude wears a frown on his face. He is always resentful and morose. He feels rejected, unwanted and is never happy. He cannot face the stress and strain of life in the right spirit. The man with the positive attitude wears a smile on his face, is buoyant, full of energy. He has the strength to face the difficulties and dangers of life, in the right spirit.

The second point of the formula is, we must not offer resistance to life. Life has given me many things. Some of them are good. Some of them are not as good. I must accept them all and make the most of them. Of course, I must not be fatalistic. I must not take things lying down. But if, in spite of my best efforts, I am not able to achieve the desired results, I must accept the situation. Acceptance is not a passive thing. To accept is to triumph over circumstances and not let them touch the joy and the peace of the soul. Resistance inevitably leads to wastage of energy which could be used to constructive ends. Do your very best to achieve your desired results, but, if in spite of your efforts, you fail, let that not depress you. The great Cosmic Power that controls the universe knows what is good for you. So accept, and rejoice!

The third point in the formula is that we must always see the good in others. The negativity that we see in others often shifts to us. If we consider the faults of others, these faults will, in due course, become part of our own nature.

REFLECT AND ACT

The statistics are frightening, whenever we consider them. The Americans are very systematic and they have statistics for all these matters. We can take America as a sample for the rest of the world. What does the picture look like there? We are told that:

- One million Americans have a heart attack each year.
- 13 million doses of tranquilisers and sedatives are prescribed yearly.
- 8 million Americans are said to have stomach ulcers.
- There are an estimated 50,000 stress-related suicides every year.
- There are 12 million alcoholics in the U.S.

Some doctors actually believe that nearly 80% of the illnesses treated in the U.S. are emotionally induced illness (EII).

What is this "Stress" that we are talking about? It is a much-used, much misused term. Dr. Hars Seyle, expert on stress-management, tells us, "Stress is the wear and tear on your body caused by life's events." It is the sum total of the body's physical, mental, and chemical reactions to circumstances which cause fear, irritation, worry, anxiety and excitement.

There are hundreds of experiences in our everyday lives which cause stress. These stress-causing events are called *stressors*. These *stressors* can create good stress (positive stress) or *distress* (negative stress). Normally, our body and its systems are conditioned to cope with *stressors*. But there is an optimum level at which each one of us can cope with stress and still function well. When the limit is exceeded, we become victims of stress.

Are you a victim of stress?
If your answer is yes, what do you intend to do about it?

IN A LIGHTER VEIN...

Experts have identified certain unusual symptoms of stress in the 21st Century:

1. You try to enter your PIN number on the microwave.

2. You haven't played Patience with real cards in years.

3. You have 15 phone numbers to reach your family of three.

4. You "chat" on the Internet several times a day with strangers from Equador/Ireland/ Qatar/etc... but you haven't spoken to your next door neighbour yet this year.

5. Your reason for not staying in touch with friends is that they don't have e-mail addresses.

6. Your idea of being organised is multiple coloured post-it notes.

7. You get most of your jokes via e-mail instead of in person.

8. When you go home after a long day at work you accidently answer the phone with "... speaking, how can I help you?"

Anger is a corroding emotion. It is a natural, but negative emotional response to stress or opposition. If we do not deal with this emotion positively, it will keep on destroying our inner self. Therefore, I say to my friends, "Burn anger before anger burns you!"

Anger is a wild fire, a forest fire which spreads from shrub to shrub, from tree to tree, consuming everything that comes in its way. In Hindi, we have a saying, "Anger is the great inflictor of sorrow, the great sinner. First it sets on fire its own mind, then the fire spreads to others."

J.P. Vaswani

ANGER MANAGEMENT

Robert Fulghum, the motivational writer, tells us that in the Solomon Islands in the South Pacific, some villagers adopt a unique strategy to fell trees. If a tree is too large to be felled with an axe, the natives cut it down by yelling at it!

Sounds incredible? But books and articles have reported this. Woodcutters with special powers creep up on a tree at dawn and suddenly start screaming at it at the top of their lungs. They continue this for thirty days. The tree dies and falls over. The theory is that the hollering kills the spirit of the tree. According to the villagers, it always works.

People yell at their spouses, their children, even at their motor cars and telephones!

I have seen modern, urban, educated people yelling at traffic signals, passing motorists and even beggars!

The Solomon Islanders may have a point. Yelling at living things does tend to kill the spirit in them. Sticks and stones may break our bones, but let us not forget, mere words can break our spirits!

WHAT IS ANGER?

Anger is a complex, physiological, human emotion that is a triggered response based on personal beliefs and expectations.

Psychologists believe that it is a cognitive, internal state of emotional reactions to life situations.

Anger management Guru, John Lee states, "Anger is equal to pain!"

When anger makes its presence felt in the body, the hormone adrenaline is secreted, the muscles tighten and the heart rate is faster.

CAUSES OF ANGER

■ Any situation that frustrates us—especially when we think someone is to blame for our unhappiness—is a cause for anger.

■ When we create in our mind a "victim" status, a feeling that we are getting a "raw deal", this too, is a potential cause of anger.

■ Psychologists find that many a time we use anger unconsciously, to accuse others in order to justify our shortcomings, or to prove to ourselves that we are better off!

DEGREES OF ANGER

■ Frustration is a short-lived reaction to minor issues that don't go our way, e.g. a flight delay, a flat tyre.

■ Anger is an internal, emotional reaction to undesirable people, their reactions or unwanted situations.

■ Righteous anger is anger best used in its corrective form, that is when used to rectify mistakes, to teach children, to correct employees, to apply law and prevent crime.

■ Aggression is anger led into action and is invariably harmful.

■ Antagonism or hatred, is anger turned chronic, and most dangerous when it is directed against a person or group and nurtured for a long period of time.

EFFECTS OF ANGER

Constant states of anger, frustration and flaring tempers over a long period of time have been known to cause the following:

■ Increased risk of cardiovascular disease
■ Reduced lung function
■ Increased blood pressure
■ Increased psychosomatic disorders
■ Disturbed stomach functions

ANGER IN THE WORKPLACE

Contemporary office scenarios, with all the mechanisation and huge amounts of information meant to simplify processes, have ironically given rise to the new age fires of ire.

In the work place anger has many new names :

- Office Rage: the terminology used to relate the rage that is experienced in the offices. People experience rage for the following reasons, so they claim:

  1. unreasonable work hours

  2. low pay

  3. stressful work

  4. demanding managers

  5. peak time travel causing stress at work

  6. information overload

  7. lack of ability to balance life between work and family life

  8. inability to constantly adapt to new technology – and the list can go on!

- Mobile Rage: a growing irritation to continuous buzzing of the mobile in offices and meetings adds to office ire.

- Net Rage: spending hours looking in vain for accurate information, with slow networks, has created net rage.

- PC rage: utter dependence on the computer which is not a superbeing, but just a fallible machine, its breakdown, and its overhauling causes frustration and anger in the office. People have been known to hurl objects at PCs in a fit of rage !

- Road rage: the growing chaotic traffic, rash driving and lack of adequate parking has given rise to the most predominant rage of our times, i.e. Road rage. Drivers experience extreme stress that causes them to pass rude comments, abuse and even assault others. The British Association for Anger Management, in a survey done in 2006, states that in the U.K. alone, 80% of all the drivers show some signs of road rage.

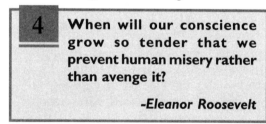

When will our conscience grow so tender that we prevent human misery rather than avenge it?

-Eleanor Roosevelt

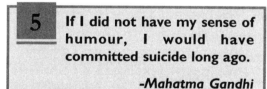

If I did not have my sense of humour, I would have committed suicide long ago.

-Mahatma Gandhi

THE MOST COMMON RESPONSES TO ANGER

The most common reactions adopted by man to infuriating situations are:

1. Expression— Giving vent to frustrations is the most frequented way of dealing with anger. People shout, yell or scream abuse. Psychiatrists tell us that it is important not to suppress anger. But then anger can become a habit and lead to constant bad temper, affecting those around us.

2. Suppression— This is what we call "bottling up" of emotions that cause havoc and it can have serious ill effects on the person's health. Such a person can also become an emotional time-bomb, because one never knows when he will explode.

3. Forgiveness— When one lets go of resentment, when one is willing to seek reconciliation with others. Forgiveness has its own rewards, and is the most peaceful way to deal with anger.

HOW DO WE STOP THE FIRE OF ANGER?

Here are 10 practical ceasefire tips that will help to stop the fires of anger!

Ceasefire Tip No. 1

Realise the Harm Caused By Anger

- Reflect over situations that have caused anger. Think about the resulting stress, the harm done to relationships and the erosion of peace. Come to terms with the fact that no matter who is right, anger is always detrimental!

- The Bhagavad Gita says, "Man is his own friend, and his own foe!" When I succumb to anger I am my own enemy, because I am poisoning my system with toxic emotions!

- Cultivate the will not to get angry! Make a promise to yourself each morning that come what may, you will not get angry.

Ceasefire Tip No. 2

See the Bigger Picture

- Think about the bigger picture. "What have we all come to this earth plane for?" Ponder upon the universal truth about existence, "What am I ?"

- Practise sitting in silence: it is then that a person realises that everything is temporary and fleeting: what exists today will vanish tomorrow. Self realisation will point to the true self, that is not the body, nor the intellect, nor the body-mind complex. *Tat twam asi! Thou art that!* When this realisation dawns, then there is no scope for wasteful emotions like anger.

Inspiration

- A man called Shivram, made a living as a motorbike salesman. He was hardworking and started clinching a lot of deals for the franchise. When he was asked what it was that made him successful, he replied, "I had made a major loss on a couple of deals when my manager told me, "Don't let it affect you, it's all evened out in the averages. In the long run the good deals offset the bad ones; and in the end, you have to see the bigger picture."

Ceasefire Tip No. 3

Practise Acceptance

- The root cause of Anger is the predominance of self will. We expect things to always go our way and are rigid to adapt to change. Anger is spurred by non acceptance of a certain situation or person.

- Let Go. Let go of situations and most importantly, let go of "fixed ideas". Look at things in a new and positive perspective.

- The surest way of acceptance is the faith that everything that happens

comes as *prasadam,* as a blessing from God.

- Rejoice in all that happens and be certain that there is a meaning of mercy in all that happens.

Inspiration

- Uday Singh had a Bachelor's degree in Commerce but no job. Desperate to earn a livelihood he managed to borrow a meagre sum of money. Finally he put up a small shop with sundry garments. On the first day a wealthy woman walked in and complained, "This place has nothing but bits and pieces," and walked out. Uday did not take offence or get angry, in fact he thanked her and the next day put up a board outside the shop saying, *Bits And Pieces* !

He began to flourish selling miscellaneous items!

Ceasefire Tip No. 4

Contact the Super Soul

- Many a time in spite of our courage of conviction and best intentions we cannot give up anger. We need to contact the Higher Power, the universal spirit or the super soul which we, for want of a better word, call God.

- God is our Divine Father and Our Divine Mother. If we appeal to God in the Mother aspect She will surely help us.

■ Pray to Her again and again, "O Mother mine, O Mother Divine! I come to Thee in a state of utter helplessness. I have Tried and I have failed. I cannot do it on my own. Let Thy strength flow into me. In Thy strength and wisdom and patience, I stand up and face every situation of life and emerge victorious! But the victory is not mine, the victory is Thine! *Jai Jai Jai Jagdamba!*"

Ceasefire Tip No. 5

Practise Empathy and Understanding

■ Whenever we become empathetic and put ourselves in the place of our offenders we become large hearted. We begin to understand why the person behaved in the way that he did.

■ It is important to remain calm and listen to the other person's point of view so the truth will begin to unfold.

■ The man with an understanding heart will not be angered.

Ceasefire Tip No. 6

Laugh it Off

■ In the event of a provoking situation, look at the humour in it and laugh it off. It will lighten the moment and ease off the tension.

Things will not seem so difficult again!

A man from the neighbouring village had come to Mullah Nasruddin's house to have a discussion with him. Since they had decided the date and time of the meet previously, the man was furious not to find Mullah there. Enraged, the man scribbled, IDIOTIC DUNCE on the Mullah's door !

When the Mullah returned he read the words on the door and immediately went to the man's house in the

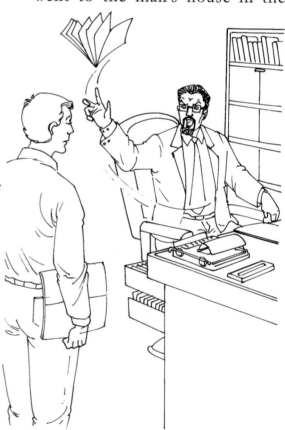

neighbouring village and knocked on the door. He apologised to the man and said, "I am sorry that I did not remember you were coming. But I realised you had come the moment I saw your signature on the door!"

Ceasefire Tip No. 7

Find Ways to Express Anger Constructively

Many people are unable to express their feelings and opinions and tend to keep seething within. This can be detrimental to one's health as all the pent up anger will manifest in some part of the body.

I read of a girl whose right arm was paralysed. On investigation it was found that she hated her sister, and was so jealous of her that she always had the urge to strike her. She suppressed the urge; but it entered her subconscious and paralysed her arm. When she went for therapy, it was brought to her notice. She gave up her jealousy and her arm was restored to normalcy.

It may be a good idea to write or maintain a journal of one's feelings or to speak to a mature colleague or spiritual elder to be able to find a way not to suppress one's anger.

Ceasefire Tip No. 8

Develop an Immunity To Criticism

- Develop a strong immunity against what people say! Make it a practice to refuse to let anything pull you down or disturb your peace of mind! Don't let people's opinions, attitudes and behaviour get the better of you.

- Start by becoming aware of how there is a reaction felt within the body when we disapprove of something. Becoming aware every time, shows how the body sends signs that it is a toxic emotion that it wants to reject.

- The body has the beautiful internal mechanism of the conscience and the soul, a higher power, working in tandem with its physiological functions. Become aware of this Higher Power within you, and let it control your moves.

- Once you start following the pattern of listening to the Voice within, and taking care of the signals sent out by your system, you will never let yourself get angry.

Ceasefire Tip No. 9

Prevention is Better Than Cure

- It is better to prevent a potentially stressful situation than to let it happen and then suffer the consequences.

Every Friday, Usha Joshi has to report for work at 8 a.m. instead of at 9. 30 a.m. for it is the day of the Weekly Review Meeting in the company, and it is her job, as the P.A. to the CEO, to ensure that everything is well organised for the meeting.

Every Friday, Usha finds it difficult to get to work, because she usually reserves the 8-9 a.m. slot to get her children ready for school. Result: she is invariably rushing to work, arriving a few minutes late, and causes anger and irritation to her colleagues.

After a couple of tension-filled Fridays, Usha's husband suggests that they wake up at 5.30 a.m. instead of at 6.30.

Usha's Fridays are no longer stressful!

Anger is an acquired habit

Many a time anger is acquired from people in our surroundings or is learnt from parents or teachers as we grow up. First we have to become aware of this. Then we can unlearn this habit consciously and more importantly make peace our goal.

Teach children by example, forgiveness and understanding. It is also important not to make our children victims of our frustration.

Children are the future of this world and if we visualise a world without war and strife; it has to begin with teaching them *today* how to give, forgive and live in peace.

Ceasefire Tip No. 10
Avoid Haste

- Mental hurry causes restlessness and anger. Avoid overwork. The very thought of a huge backlog of work causes agitation.

- Do your work lovingly, gently, quietly.

A clerk at an office had to do the mechanical job of filing everyday. On one particular day he had a lot of files to organise. A friend asked him, "You must be tired and overworked today. Isn't that a lot of filing to do in a day?"

The clerk replied, "I concentrate on only one file at a time, the one that is before me, so I never feel overworked."

You are not your emotions! They are just a part of you. They are just how you feel!

Visual Exercise:

Detach yourself from the emotions and watch them from a distance. Identify and label each thought. Categorise them into wanted and unwanted thoughts. "Delete" the unwanted thoughts from your system

PRACTICAL SUGGESTIONS

To sum up: Here are a few Practical Suggestions that will help you to burn anger before it ignites you!

1. The best and surest way of controlling anger is the way of self-realisation. Once you realise who you are you will never be angry. This implies identification with our Highest Self.

2. Develop the will to control anger. Realise the uselessness of anger. We may not harm the person at whom we feel angry but we surely harm ourselves when we are angry.

3. Accept every incident and accident as God's will. Rejoice in whatever His will brings to you. You will then arrive at a stage where nothing will upset you and make you angry.

4. Seek the help of God – the Mother Divine – to control your anger. Without His grace, you can achieve nothing.

5. Avoid occasions. Whenever you find yourself in a situation which makes you angry, turn away from it.

6. Avoid haste – for haste is the mother of anger, even as hatred is its father.

7. Whenever you feel anger approaching, keep your mouth shut and your lips sealed. When you speak, speak sweetly, lovingly, softly, gently.

8. If you are unable to keep quiet, hum to yourself a simple tune. This will help you to relax and remain calm.

9. When angry, drink a glass or two of cold water. Or go out and take a brisk walk, or run or jog. Exercise will burn up your negative emotional energy.

10. Count upto ten, or if you are very angry, count upto hundred.

REFLECT AND ACT

For years, psychologists have recommended that we 'blow off steam' when we are angry – without physically or emotionally harming anyone. We've been told that hitting a punching bag or throwing our fist into a pillow will help us to ease the tension that is building up within us.

The latest research seems to indicate that this is not as effective as it may sound. Such a system of quick release through an emergency valve may actually increase your anger.

In a study conducted by psychologists from Iowa State University and Case Western Reserve, 700 college students who were insulted by an unseen partner, were placed in a situation where they could direct a blast of noise at the person who they believed insulted them.

The control group tried to let off steam by hitting a punching bag for two minutes. It didn't matter. In fact, their responses became even more angry. The findings were reported in the Journal of Personality and Social Psychology.

Perhaps the best way to reduce anger is to take a few deep breaths and let your negative feelings dissipate slowly. Blowing your top — even if no one hears you — is tough on your own nervous system.

> **What is your way of dealing with anger?**
> **Are you likely to change your strategy to deal with this negative emotion now?**

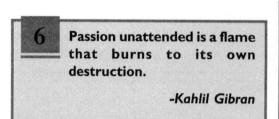

6 Passion unattended is a flame that burns to its own destruction.

-*Kahlil Gibran*

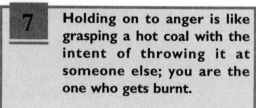

7 Holding on to anger is like grasping a hot coal with the intent of throwing it at someone else; you are the one who gets burnt.

-*Gautama Buddha*

In A Lighter Vein...

In New York City, a taxi driver hit and scraped a red BMW while veering across four lanes of traffic to pick up a customer. The two drivers got out to examine the damage.

The taxi driver was a short man of Middle Eastern origin, the BMW driver, a hulking white giant.

As the cabbie approached, the BMW driver grabbed him by the shirt and hoisted him off the ground. There, at eye level with the cabbie's feet dangling in the air, the BMW owner began screaming, every third sentence being, "This is your lucky day!"

Eventually, the cabbie was lowered back to terra firma, but then, the BMW guy asked him, "Don't you want to know why this is your lucky day?"

He then proceeded to answer his own question:

"Because I'm on my way to an anger management class and I don't dare show up with blood on my shirt!"

Fear casts its dark shadow over our lives at one time or another. We are prone to fear almost instinctively. Neither the highest nor the lowest of us is exempt from fear. The most powerful nations fear their rivals and neighbours. Politicians are afraid of losing elections. Students are afraid of failing in examinations. Mothers are afraid about their children's safety… The list is endless.

Fear is the one mark that characterises us, children of a sceptical age. We are afraid of the future, afraid of poverty, afraid of unemployment, afraid of dishonour and disgrace, afraid of disease and death – it seems to me that sometimes, we are afraid of life itself!

We live in fear; we work in fear; we walk in fear; we talk in fear. We move through life from one fear to another, crushed beneath the weight of a woeful existence!

J.P. Vaswani

FEAR MANAGEMENT

In recognition of his dedication to the *Journal*, William Randolph Hearst, the news magnate, once offered columnist Arthur Brisbane a six-month vacation on full pay. When Brisbane declined to accept, Hearst understandably asked him why.

Brisbane provided two good reasons: "The first is that if I quit writing for six months, I am afraid that it might damage the circulation of your newspapers," he explained. "The second reason is an even greater fear – that it might not!"

WHAT IS FEAR?

Fear is the devastating emotion that has plagued our modern age.

- The encyclopedia describes Fear as "a survival mechanism that usually occurs in response to negative stimuli."

- Fear comes in different shades. It varies in degree from Apprehension, Worry, Anxiety, Phobia, and Fright – to abject Terror.

- Fear can be positive or negative: Positive Fear is that aspect of fear which acts as a signal to warn against danger or that which motivates us to improve our performance or to prevent our downfall. A fear of not being accepted by society causes us to conform to norms and discipline our lives. These kind of fears are considered necessary!

  Negative fears are imaginary, exaggerated, illogical and extremely corrosive. These fears cause us to anticipate imaginary, non-existent problems and blur our vision of reality. They are barriers between people and reality. Negative fears are either conditioned through people and situations or acquired through traumatic experiences.

- When fed, these negative fears grow to monstrous proportions and don the form of anxiety and depression.

UNDERSTAND FEAR

- It is normal and human to have real fears that help us to deal with the everyday challenges of life. They foster a sense of self-preservation. If it was not for these fears we would be walking into speeding cars, putting our hands into fire, rebelling against authority, etc. These fears are in proportion to the dangers posed. For example, if one hears a thunderstorm, sees lightning and stays indoors from fear of being struck by lightning, then it is a fear caused by the survival instinct!

- It is the unreal, the negative fears that are not in proportion to the danger threat that turn into phobias.

> 8 Nothing in life is to be feared. It is only to be understood!
>
> -Emerson

How true are the words of Rudyard Kipling, "Of all the liars in the world, sometimes the worst are your own fears." Taking up the example previously cited, if a man becomes so obsessed with the fear of being struck by lightning that he cannot even venture out in a light drizzle and has negative imaginings of himself being electrocuted, he has a psychological problem! Facts always point that more deaths are wrought by fear of calamities than the calamities themselves.

It has been found in a study by the Massachusets Institute of Technology that the chances of death caused by lightning are one in 1.9 million. In such situations one is reminded of an acronym of FEAR - False Evidence Appearing Real.

WHY DO WE FEAR?

- Psychiatrists tell us that the fear of falling and the fear of loud noises are present in babies when they are born. Fears like these are innate.

- Many fears are learned. They are caused by conditioning from parents, peers, educators, media, society and culture. They are also a product of social standards. They are absorbed by the pattern in which people around us react to dangers, calamities or even simple problems. Fears of darkness, spiders, plane crashes, fear of illness, fear of drowning, etc. are common examples. Fear of the unknown is a fear that is most common.

- Some fears are acquired as a reaction to some unhappy, childhood incidents. For example, a child locked up in a room as a punishment may develop Claustrophobia, a fear of enclosures.

- Fears can also develop in the later years as a repercussion to some trauma. For example if a person sees a car crash, he becomes fearful of driving.

9 We must build dikes of courage to hold back the flood of fear.

-**Martin Luther King. Jr.**

THE ROOTS OF FEAR

"The mind is its own place," wrote Milton, "and in itself can create a heaven of hell, a hell of heaven."

There is great meaning in these words. If fear has to be wiped out, it has to be uprooted from the mind.

A turbulent mind causes uneasiness, fear and anxiety. The mind has to be stilled and its restless energy must be harnessed and channelised into constructive thoughts and plans.

The conquered mind is a source of poise and serenity. When there is inner calm, people and events don't shock a person.

The desire for things to always go our way, leads to disappointments and fears! Selfish thoughts should be replaced by positive, accepting and selfless thoughts.

2500 years back, when people approached Buddha with their problems, his solution was the same. They said to him, "We have fears and worries! What should we do?"

"If you want to be happy and fearless, then train your mind!" he answered.

Each One To His Fear!

Dozens of surveys conducted in a cross-section of different countries, genders, professions and ages reveal that fears are today a part of everyone's emotional baggage.

The irony of the matter is that what may be a very real fear to one may be absurd to another and may seem unthinkable to the third. A brief view of the diverse fears' impact across the world are like this:

- Britons are most afraid of terrorist attacks. Italians are afraid of radiation from mobiles. Americans are afraid of another recession. Most of the educated people over the world have one common fear and that is the fear of global warming.
- Among other fears the fear of spiders, fear of electrocution through lightning and the fear of plane crashes are predominant in the Western world.
- Indians are considered to be comparatively free from fear.
- Men are most afraid of losing their jobs or going bankrupt.
- Women are most afraid of relationship problems.

- Western teenagers are most afraid of losing their social acceptance, but more Indian teenagers are afraid of not performing well in exams.

- Older people are afraid of loneliness and illness.

- Most people are afraid of death, especially the death of a loved one. Almost all people are afraid of the unknown!

Because of the diversity experienced in fears one can be consoled of the fact that there is no universal reality common to all fears.

THE EFFECTS OF FEAR

- When we allow fear to grow, it paralyses our faculties. It makes us feel powerless against situations.

- Fear causes immense physical damage, ranging from acidity and ulcers to fainting. In many cases, extreme shock and fear in the form of terror has even caused cardiac arrests.

- Fear causes palpitations in many people.

- Panic attacks bring symptoms such as choking, numbess, lack of breath, nausea, sweating, etc.

TACKLING FEAR HEAD ON

Identify Fear

- The first step to deal with fear is awareness. It is very important to identify fear and feel its presence in your body and mind. Every situation that triggers off fear should be recognised.

- Understand what you fear! Analyse it –break it down! What is it? Is it a monster that is real or a fabrication of the mind? Is it rational?

One way to look at fear is to observe its incidence. If one person is afraid of the dark and another is not, the second person is afraid of cats and

the third is not, then that means there is nothing in the dark nor in the cats that is inherently fear causing! The fear is only our response! Therefore once it is established that fear is irrational, its tyranny on the mind will be broken.

A practical exercise to face fear

Here is a simple exercise, that will relieve your load from the fears that you carry:

Make a list of the fears that you are feeling now, and face your worst fears right in the eye. They could be something like this:

- I am afraid of another stock market crash
- I am afraid to ask my manager for a raise
- I am afraid to delegate work to my subordinates
- I am afraid I may not get a suitable job
- I am afraid no one will marry me
- I am afraid that my wife no longer loves me
- I am afraid that my son is going to fail his exam

Now go through each fear and read aloud for each of them: *I have created this fear! It exists only in my mind and now I am willing to let it go! I am more powerful than my fears! My future is bright and beautiful!*

Fears are the thoughts that we have allowed the mind to think! Get on the driver's seat of your mind and spurn away your fears with constant positive affirmations.

Realise the Futility of Fear
Sandhya sat down to take instructions from her new boss. He asked her to make a list of all the unfinished jobs that had to be attended to. The list was enormous! Sandhya's heart sank in apprehension.

Now, the boss handed the list back to her and told her to divide the tasks into two categories: He asked her to mark "F" against the tasks she feared she could not do, as well as those whose deadlines caused her apprehensions: she was to mark "H" against the tasks that she was happy and enthusiastic to do.

He explained to her that fear inhibits our true potential and any work done with fear cannot be fruitful.

Realising the harm caused by fear is a concrete step in the direction to overcome fear.

When fear grips us, our faculty of reason, our performance level, our efficiency and ability to make decisions are all lost!

PRACTISE THE PRESENT

All fears are negative anticipations of the future.

The fears about the future are triggered by unhappy events that occurred in the past.

Thus past and future are inextricably linked in a chain of expectation, fear and despair that binds us to negative thoughts.

The only escape from the past and future is the present. Therefore if e is always aware of the present oment, with thoughts focused on the re-and-now, there will be no time to r.

Getting overwhelmed by fears of at-will-happen also takes away the ength to deal with the problems of present.

In this connection, it is important understand the difference between nning for the future and fearing the ure! Plan the schedule of the near ure without imagining or expecting verse results.

e Beasts of the Past and Future

A man venturing through a jungle he Western Ghats of Maharashtra, ddenly saw a tiger on the prowl. The er sniffed and leapt in the direction the man. The man ran for his life, ng chased by the ferocious animal! reached a point where he would er be devoured by the beast or had jump into a shrub at the edge of a f. The cliff was not too steep but uld serve to save him from the tiger. decided to take this chance. He ked down to calculate the risk of a ip down the cliff, when to his shock

he saw a pack of hungry wolves looking up at him.

Either at the top or at the bottom of the cliff, death was certain. He realised his only chance at life was to hang on to the shrub for dear life. He chose not to look up or down, which was when he realised he was hanging on to a tree with juicy red fruits. He plucked one and then another and

came to the conclusion that they were the sweetest fruits he had ever eaten.

In the meanwhile, the animals waited for long and then gave up and wandered away.

The story seeks to bring out the importance of the present moment and the task that lies in front of us. The wild beasts signify the past and the future. The rule to remember is that whenever one is intimidated by the past or the future, the only relief that one can find is in living in the present moment.

Convert Fear into a Catalyst

John McCain states in his book, *Why Courage Matters,* "Fear is the opportunity for courage, not proof of cowardice."

Fear should be made a catalyst to overcome the weaknesses of the mind. The purpose of our existence is to come to terms with our true nature without our illusions.

For instance, if a person is afraid of drowning, he must use it as an opportunity to strengthen his will power and go ahead and learn to swim.

Such positive actions help to free the mind from self-imposed shackles.

Surinder had a devastating childhood. He had been witness to his father's painful death and his older sister's accident. He grew up with an anxiety disorder. He suffered from an obsessive fear of death and simply could not enjoy the blessings of life.

As he approached his teenage, his mother, a woman of faith, spoke to him about death and why it is never to be feared. True it is that death occurs but once, and that too at its appointed time. Yet the world lives in perpetual fear of death.

Surinder began to look at his life from a fresh perspective. He began thinking about the many things that he had been blessed with. He realised that his mother was a greater victim of circumstances, but was fearless and loving. She was a source of strength to him. He learnt from her example to put the past behind him, to become fearless. He realised the transient nature of life and decided to convert his fear to courage. He decided to live a rich and fruitful life.

Accept Change and Uncertainty

Man is threatened by that which he cannot control. That is what causes him to fall into the deep abyss of fear.

But such is the law of the universe, that man is subject to a power greater than his own. Change and uncertainty are inevitable in human life!

Fear of change, fear of the unknown is a form of resistance to life. It is like going against a strong current.

One thing we can do is to relinquish all mental resistance to things we cannot control and simply accept all that comes our way.

A better remedy to wipe out fear is not just to accept, but to rejoice in all that comes on our pathway in the journey called life, in the secure knowledge that it happens by the will of God!

Anchor your Ship

Most of us are unsecured like floating ships! We need to latch onto a Power that is greater than ours.

This is because fear is persistent and potent, and we may not have the strength to deal with it alone.

We need to anchor our ship to the Eternal Power, whom for want of a better word we call God! For He is the Source of everything!

Until we establish a firm relationship with Him, it is very

beneficial to begin repeating a prayer every time we are in a panic attack!

I often repeat the following prayer from the verses of my beloved Master, Sadhu Vaswani:

> The sea is vast, my skiff is small:
> I trust in Thee, who guard'st all!

The spoken word, the uttered prayer, has the power to fight all evil, temptation, anger and fear!

I also draw strength from the words of Ella Wheeler Wilcox :

> I will not doubt though all my ships at sea
> Come drifting home with broken masts and sails
> I shall believe in the Hand which never fails
> From seeking evil worketh good for me:
> And though I weep because those sails are battered,
> Still will I cry, while my best hopes lie shattered,
> "I trust in Thee!"

Seek Inspiration

- All men have some form of fear or other. Did people like Mahatma Gandhi, Martin Luther King, Helen Keller and Swami Vivekananda have fears? Yes! They too had fears, but they used fear as a motivator to overcome obstacles. They transformed fears into will power and subjugated the mind. The lives of illustrious people speak of tremendous challenges that they faced. It was their courage and their sheer grit to thwart fear that made them what they were.

- Fearlessness has been the hallmark of the world's greatest intellects, martyrs and saints. That is why Socrates drank the *hemlock* unruffled. That is why Christ allowed himself to be crucified. That is why the Mahatma faced his assassin's bullets with the Name of God on his lips. These great souls cultivated the will to be unafraid, to overcome fear at all costs.

- Seeking inspiration from great lives will help us to see that the problems we face are so trivial and the fears we have are empty.

- The Reverend Billy Graham has this to say, "Courage is contagious. When a brave man takes a stand, the spines of others are stiffened."

- Make the lives of the great ones real in your life and fear will become an obsolete word in your dictionary.

THE INTREPID SWAMI

Swami Vivekananda was a champion of courage and strength. While he was in the United States Of America, he addressed large audiences about the wisdom of India's *rishis* and sages. He said that the way of the heroes is the way of fearlessness in the face of calamity, even in the face of death.

A group of young unbelievers wanted to put him to the test. They invited him to deliver a lecture and he gladly agreed. He spoke at the meet about faith in God. He said that a man of faith was fearless in the face of danger and difficulty.

Suddenly loud gunshots were heard in the hall. Bullets were shot in the direction of the Swami, just missing his ears. An uproar arose from hysterical people in the hall. They were screaming, fainting and running berserk. But amidst the chaos one person was unperturbed and undaunted. Swami Vivekananda stood fearless and still. He knew that if the bullet was not meant to hurt him it would never touch him, and if it was meant to harm him, it would seek him through a hundred shields and guards.

Some of the superlative insights from Swami Vivekananda are, "Strength is life, weakness is death. Weakness is the one cause of suffering. Because we are weak, we suffer."

When we read the lives of such heroes of humanity, we too, can imbibe the same quality of courage!

FEAR AND FAITH CANNOT COEXIST!

- Fear and Faith repel each other. Where there is true faith there can never be fear. Therefore the best antidote to fear is faith.

- Faith is the most powerful emotion known to man. Faith is not the blind belief that God grants all our prayers : Faith means knowing that all that happens is part of a Divine plan. Faith means believing without doubt that everything was perfect in the past, that everything is perfect in the present and that everything will be perfect in the future. It is faith in the universe and all that is truth and virtuous in this world or faith in that Power which for want of a better word, we call God.

- The Persian poet Sadi said, "I fear God, and next to God, I fear most of all, him who fears Him not."

- When a little child is thrown up into the air by his father, the child giggles with joy! For he knows full well that when his father has thrown him up, he will surely catch him! That is because the child has implicit and utter faith in his father.

- This is true for us with our Divine Father, if he puts us to test it is He who will hold us! If our faith in Him is unconditional and absolute, He will never let us down!

Let God Run Your Life!

One of Oliver Cromwell's officers was given to the habit of constant anxiety and worry. His faithful servant was a pious man, who wished to help his worrisome master.

He asked his master, "Is it not true that the Lord ran this world long before you came into it?"

"Sure, he did", replied the master instantly.

"You believe that he will run it after you have left, don't you?"

Again, the officer nodded in acceptance.

"Then why don't you stop worrying and let Him run it while you are in it?" asked the servant.

PRACTICAL SUGGESTIONS

Here are seven steps on the road that leads from fear to fearlessness:

1. Convince yourself that nothing that you fear is as bad as the fear itself. To be afraid is the worst thing that can happen to you.

2. Be sure you want to give up the thing you are afraid of. You must have the will to be free.

3. Never forget that fear is a kind of atheism.

4. With God all things are possible.

5. To receive the Power of God, learn to relax in His Presence.

6. Do not be afraid of what may happen tomorrow.

7. Go out of yourself and bring help and comfort to others.

REFLECT AND ACT

Hendrik Egberg says that fear is like a big roadblock, the massive wall in the middle of the road, that keeps you from getting what you want.

He suggests the following exercise to break through the wall of fear.

1. Take small steps at first: for example, if you are afraid to speak in public, start off by saying hello to strangers; then try "chatting" on internet forums; and then try joining conversations in parties. So, identify your fear. Then make a plan with some smaller steps you can take to gradually lessen your discomfort.

2. Get Motivated: One way to get moving is to replace some of your negative thoughts with clear, positive reasons to get going. Take just five minutes. Take out a piece of paper and a pen. And write down all the wonderful ways you can come up with to overcome negative thinking patterns: visualise how making this change will improve your life. Writing down all the wonderful things you will gain in your life by overcoming this fear can be powerful. Focus on those positive things to get motivated and inspired. Revisit your page of paper when you feel discouraged, uncomfortable or afraid.

3. See failure and rejection in a new light: Often it is easier not to do something because we fear failure and rejection. We may fear failure when starting on a

new career-path. And rejection from friends, family and the people around us if we fail. Or we might be afraid of being rejected when asking people for help.

However, the definition of failure we are brought up with in society might not be the best and most useful to have. If you look at the most successful people, you quickly notice that they have a very different response to failure. They don't take failure or rejection that seriously. They know it is not the end of the world if they fail. Instead they look at each failure and see the good part about it : what they can learn from it and improve next time.

4. Be in the *now*: what this means is to keep yourself steadily in the *now*, not letting your thoughts and emotions run away to the future or the past. That does not mean that you don't make plans, of course. But being in the *now* means not getting your mind stuck in a kind of psychological and emotional headspace that is placed in the past or future. It means not dwelling on what has gone wrong before and what could go wrong tonight or tomorrow. Such thinking will only blow up your fear to the point where you feel unable to do anything.

Instead, make your plans. Then just be and don't think about the future. Focus on the *now* and what needs to be done *now*. The future will be the *now* soon enough. And when you arrive there, it will be much easier to get things done when you have only a minimal amount of stress and fear within your mind.

5. Redefine Yourself: You are the architect of your own destiny! You are what you think you are! You have to be willing to change, that's all it takes to make a new you. Keep at these techniques. Practise each one regularly. No one can do it for you. But if you persist with these efforts, you can make what may seem to you to be big progress, very quickly indeed. And when you get used to it and these attitudes and habits become more and more habitual, you will start to practise them naturally.

IN A LIGHTER VEIN...

It was February 2003, and America was on the verge of a war with Iraq. Tension was almost tangible in the corridors of power. Secretary of State Colin Powell, was caught as it were, in the eye of the storm. Someone informed him, that, notwithstanding the stress, President George W. Bush was in bed by ten o'clock every night and slept like a baby. "I sleep like a baby, too," Powell replied. "Every two hours I wake up screaming!"

Good health is the greatest of all gifts, the choicest of all blessings – for without it, we cannot enjoy any of our other faculties and blessings…

Good health is the basis of all that we value and cherish in human life – success, achievement, financial prosperity, emotional security, and above all, spiritual unfoldment and inner peace.

J.P. Vaswani

HEALTH MANAGEMENT

Indian businessmen and managers worship Lakshmi, the Goddess of wealth, with great fervour. But few of them know that Dhanvantri, hailed as the Physician of the Gods, also appeared out of the *samudra manthan* – the churning of the ocean by the *asuras* and *devas,* described in the *Puranas.* Dhanvantri is depicted as an *avatar* of Vishnu with four hands, holding medical herbs in one hand and a pot containing rejuvenating nectar – *amrita* – in another.

We would all do well to remember: Health is a very important form of wealth!

IN QUEST OF GOOD HEALTH...

There is more cause for concern in the health sector in today's advanced society, than ever before. With a complex lifestyle and simplified work processes, we have more and more health problems! With more money being spent on research and development, and greater advancements in medicine, there are more cases of heart attacks, ulcer and diabetes! It has been observed that in the last ten years there has been a sharp rise in the incidence of depression, much reduced levels of immunity, a great fall in forbearance and a growing dissatisfaction with life!

It is time to wake up and take a look at where we are heading! Is good health our prerogative?

The answer is an emphatic –Yes! Good health is our birthright! Therefore it is important to understand what good health is and how one can achieve it!

Good health is the physical, mental, social, spiritual and emotional well being of a human being. Man is a complex fabrication of intellect, matter and spirit. His mind, body and soul are intertwined, inter dependant.

Therefore health should not be considered as a reference to only the physical state of an individual.

The wisdom of the Bhagavad Gita points to the soul as the essence of man. Lord Krishna says to his dear disciple, "Arjuna, remember that you are not the body. The body is only a garment that you wear." This great truth is expressed in different ways by various seers and sages through the centuries.

To live a truly complete and healthy life, we should adopt a holistic approach. Mental balance, emotional stability, humanitarianism, fitness of the body and strength of spirit should be our goal.

It is also important to note that being healthy is a means and not an end. Today, city dwellers have started treating dieting, exercise and fitness as mere aids to looking good. They seem to forget that being fit is basic to being healthy.

One should aim to be healthy to be able to live a wholesome, happy, harmonious and fruitful life! And above all to be able to fulfill one's purpose in life.

- Good health is a choice we make. It is not imposed on us from without.

- To be healthy choose tranquility instead of stress, choose hard work instead of lethargy, choose moderation instead of indulgence and calm instead of impulse!

- You can change your attitude to change your health. With the exception of genetic and accidental health problems, most other forms of illness are self-induced.

Heal Yourself Prescriptions

The following therapies are tried and tested solutions to keep body, mind and soul healthy.

Therapy No. 1

Happiness Therapy

The cause of disease can be traced from the break up of the word itself: disease. That which is not at ease. Therefore illness is caused by lack of ease, joy and happiness.

There is no better health booster than happiness. Happiness is a choice one has to make! Although circumstances may not be what we wish for, the choice to think happy thoughts is our prerogative.

Studies show that happiness or related states like hopefulness, optimism and contentment appear to reduce the severity of cardiovascular disease, diabetes, hypertension, colds and upper respiratory infections.

New researches at the University College of London have linked everyday happiness with healthier levels of body chemicals, such as the hormone cortisol, etc.

Happiness is best fostered by positive thinking and laughter. Clinical psychologist Jane Wardle says, "Perhaps laughter truly is the best medicine."

The incidence of health problems of the present times can be related to the lack of mirth in our daily lives. Dr. Michael Titze, a German psychologist points out an astounding fact: In the 1950's people used to laugh at an average of 18 minutes a day. In contrast these days we laugh for not more than 5 minutes a day!

Laughter is a natural, restorative tonic. A French neurologist, Henry Rubenstein, states in his findings that just one minute of hearty laughter can give the body an equivalent of 45 minutes of therapeutic relaxation.

Therapy No. 2

Nutrition Therapy

Nutrition plays a big role in the maintenance of good health.

We would all do well to remember a simple truth about the human constitution: we are what we eat.

A plethora of research has been done in the field of nutrition to point to attributes of various foods and their impact on our health.

Some of the fundamental truths about food are universal and apply to all of mankind. The following facts about food and fasting can be adapted into our life styles to avoid disease.

FACTS ABOUT FOOD

- It is very important to eat food at the right time. Breakfast should never be missed.

- It has been found that people who eat a good breakfast are less likely to be obese and diabetic than those who don't.

- One should avoid emotional eating. Many people eat when they are bored, stressed, anxious, and need a sense of security. This causes them to binge on the wrong things and in huge quantities.

- Most people eat to finish the plate. One should take small helpings and listen to the body's signals. One should stop just before one is full.

- Too much junk food, refined foods, etc. make the digestion sluggish. Excessive sugar causes indigestion.

- Food should be heated well before eating. If cold food is eaten then the digestive juices are strained to warm the food before it can be metabolised. That is why cold drinks are harmful. They weaken the digestive system.

- Eating just before sleeping gets the stomach strained and gets it working through the sleeping hours.

- In times when refined foods are a predominant ingredient in most preparations, it is very important to add more dietary fiber in all that we eat.

- It has been proved through Kirlian Photography (one that captures vibrations and auras of objects and people), that the vibration of food is raised manifold when prayers are offered before the food. Therefore the food that is empty due to pesticides and excessive cooking can be made **more** wholesome and nutritious by asking for God's grace and thanking Him.

- Non-vegetarian food has been proved to be cancerous.

- People who eat non-vegetarian food are eating second hand nutrition. What this means is that nutrition comes from vegetables, fruits, nuts and grains and is consumed by the animals that are killed for their meat.

- Foods of flesh only build up fats but never help to give vitality and radiance to the body.

- Pulses, nuts and lentils are a source of high protein for vegetarians and are sufficient to meet the requirement of a human being.

- Animal diseases like bird flu, mad cow disease, etc. are on the rise and it is best to avoid eating meat even for health reasons.

- Dr. Kellogg, a famous vegetarian states, "When we eat vegetarian food, we don't have to worry about what kind of disease the food died of."

- Animal food is unacceptable on three grounds humanitarian, aesthetic and hygienic.

- Complete attention should be given to the food that we are eating, without letting the mind wander off in many directions.

- One should be aware of the taste, the texture and flavour of what one is eating. Chewing and masticating the food should be done with full consciousness. The focus on the food should be such that each bite should be a new one. One should eat in a calm, unhurried manner.

- One should eat with positive thoughts in mind. While eating if we think negative thoughts then our food will turn into poison.

FACTS ABOUT FASTING

- Fasting means abstinence from food for a few hours or days.

- Binging between meals, munching out of boredom and insecurity takes its toll on the digestion. Sedentary lifestyle, lack of exercise, wrong and large quantities of food that are consumed overburden the digestive tract. Fasting rids the body of such fats, toxins and sets right the dysfunction of the organs.

- By fasting our overworked digestive system receives much needed rest.

- Fasting is known to be the best way to cleanse and detoxify the system. It also helps in developing discipline and will power.

- Occasional fasting is good for all of us. Only weak people and those with debilitating diseases should avoid fasting.

- *Langanam parama aushadam*- fasting is the supreme medicine as per ancient traditions and the Vedas. All the major religions of the world propagate fasting.

■ Animals and even children automatically avoid food when they are unwell. This is because fasting is nature's way of treating any disorder that afflicts us.

Therapy No. 3

Emotions therapy

Psychologist and author Daniel Goleman coined the term EQ or emotional quotient. He compared emotional intelligence to cognitive intelligence. He found that when our emotions are not in balance, we get the same results as when our brain is not functioning well. Then we do unproductive and damaging things. Thus when our emotions are imbalanced, our body is at the receiving end of harmful signals.

Positive emotions like love, caring, sharing, altruism, etc. have a powerful effect on the human psyche. They have been known to have immense healing power. On the other hand, negative emotions create an imbalance in the body leading to ill-health.

In recent years we have been introduced to the concept of emotionally induced illness (EII). Specialists believe that EII is responsible for as much as 95% of all illnesses.

Anger, fear, envy, jealousy, worry, grief, shame, guilt, etc. are the negative emotions that are potentially hazardous to health. In fact the seven deadly sins of Christian theology – i.e. pride, covetousness, lust, anger, gluttony, envy and sloth – can make one seriously ill. More than one of them can make a person ill for long time and a group of them can be fatal.

Have you ever worried yourself sick? Does thinking about a mango slice make your mouth water? Does the thought of an incident in the past make you cry? This goes to prove that emotional and physical states are inter-dependant. So well is the body-mind connection fabricated that every emotion we feel finds its effect on some function of our body.

Therefore, we must make every effort to keep our emotions in balance; let petty things go, keep no grudges, think happy thoughts and choose the company of calm and happy people.

Therapy No. 4

Oxygen Therapy

Of all the requirements of the human body, oxygen is the most vital. After that come water and food.

Prana, breath is the vital force of life.

City life compels us to breathe polluted air, which deprives us of pure oxygen.

Lack of pure oxygen puts our bodily functions under great stress. The lungs become sluggish and are unable to provide oxygen to the heart and the brain. Then the organs slow down in their efficiency.

The American Lung Association has stated that up to 50% of all illnesses are either caused or aggravated by polluted air.

Therefore it becomes extremely crucial that we practise breathing deeply. We have become accustomed to breathing at very shallow levels. We must breathe at the level of the belly. Also, it is important to breathe only through the nose and not through the mouth. It is only through the nostrils that the air gets purified and filtered.

Another way to increase oxygenation is to spend more time in the early hours of the morning with nature. The trees let out huge amounts of pure oxygen.

Pranayama, a systematic deep breathing yogic exercise passed on from our ancient sages, when practiced regularly, provides high amounts of oxygen to all parts of the body. It has been proved to be curative because the constant influx of oxygen also opens up blocked nerve and blood vessel pathways in the body.

Therapy No. 5

Nature Therapy

Nature is the mother of humanity; alas, we have become alienated from her.

"Living in the lap of nature" takes us closer to our true identity.

Hundreds of studies conducted by experts point to the stress-relieving aspect of nature. Spending time in nearby natural locations like parks and lakes, or even in the wilderness has been proven to increase physical energy and effective relaxation.

Nature offers a sense of fascination and wonderment, which makes one feel like a little child! This feeling instantly relieves fatigue.

In a study done by Steven and Rachel Kaplan, of Michigan University, they found that after 45 minutes of stressful mental work, a walk in a natural area led to better, calming recovery than a walk in an urban area, or reading magazines and listening to music.

In a finding by Roger Ulrich and others, it is shown that just a view of nature from a hospital room window facilitates recovery from surgery. Likewise, a scenic view from an office room improves work performance and increases job satisfaction.

Studies by other researchers point that children who are exposed to even little patches of green in the cluttered areas of urban settings have shown great improvement in attention spans.

Therefore, to be healthy, spend time, exercise and breathe in the loving, open arms of nature.

LIVING IN TANDEM WITH NATURE

- After the Tsunami that hit southeast Asia and killed more than 300 thousand people in 2004, many studies were conducted to find if any warning signals were felt. It was found that a couple of tourists from England who had studied Tsunamis could only see warning signs a few minutes beforehand. But the astonishing fact of all was that nature had warned her children beforehand!

- It was found that very few animals died in the massive Tsunami. Elephants, buffaloes, tigers and smaller animals all managed to move to higher ground in time. Scientists think that they sensed sound waves and changes in air pressure in advance of the deadly wave. This premonition gave them time to escape.

We too are nature's children, but we have stopped listening to her whispers. We too can be intuitive, if only we connect with the universe.

Therefore we must tune ourselves with nature and live our lives in synchronicity with her. We must cease to abuse nature for our superficial needs.

Therapy No. 6

Lifestyle Therapy

Urban and metropolitan dwellers have redefined lifestyle. Lifestyle today means to many, the standard of living, the attire, the aura of style they exude. But lifestyle simply means "the way we live". It is the way we conduct our lives. In the past two decades, gradually, we have adapted ourselves to a life of show and pretence, not realising that we are harming our health, mental balance and equilibrium.

In a recent study, it was found that 7 out of 10 diseases are lifestyle related.

In what ways can we improve our lifestyle?

1. Say NO to alcohol and drugs.
2. Sleep early and rise early.
3. Say NO to junk.
4. Avoid places that fill you with negativity, places that are claustrophobic.
5. Plant more trees.
6. Always maintain correct posture. Do not be sloppy.
7. Take care of old people at home and in your family; always respect the elderly.
8. Avoid too much usage of mobiles. Keep them only for emergencies.
9. Stay away from too much radiation from gadgets like televisions, computers and laptops.
10. Spend some time everyday in silence and prayer. If possible, go to a *satsang* (Spiritual fellowship) at least once a day.
11. Help others. This makes you heartier and healthier.
12. Let things pass. Nothing in life is worth causing anxiety or stress.
13. Develop a healthy sense of humour. Laugh at life and its oddities but never at others.
14. Drink plenty of water. At least 8 to 10 glasses of water are required to wash out the toxins from the body.

Therapy No. 7

Discipline Therapy

Indulgence is the cause of disease. Gluttony, lust and self-gratification are known to be the deadliest sins of mankind.

Self discipline is the exercise of spiritual muscles.

It was Mahatma Gandhi who said, "Many are the keys to good health. No doubt they are essential; but the one thing needful above all others is *brahmacharya,* celibacy."

Practicing celibacy, self-restraint and self-denial implies conquest over passions. With that one conserves one's life-force energy. One also grows in spiritual evolution and develops intuition.

Sadhu Vaswani said, *"Brahmacharya* is walking and moving with God." Literally also it means living with *Brahman*, the Absolute, the Divine Self. *Brahmacharya* can be practiced even by *grihastas* (married men).

Therapy No. 8

Exercise Therapy

Exercise in any form is necessary for keeping the body and mind finely tuned.

Exercise slows down aging, improves metabolism, reduces stress, improves muscle tone, improves immunity, helps elimination, raises the performance of all the organs, and provides essential oxygen supply to the vital organs of the body.

Increased supply of oxygen to the body puts greater energy at our disposal. Thus we will have added vigour and enthusiasm to face life and combat illness.

Exercises which are aerobic, i.e. ones that provide increased oxygenation, are very essential, like swimming, walking, running, jogging, tennis, etc.

Walking is the queen of all exercises, because it activates and stimulates all the organs of the body. One must walk to one's destination whenever possible.

Yoga brings wonderful benefits of helping to calm down the mind and energise the body. It improves breathing and tones up the muscles.

If one exercises for at least 10 to 15 minutes per day, it is sufficient to aid elimination and keep the body fit.

When one sweats while exercising, it is known to wash out at least one-third of the toxins built up in the system.

Therapy No. 9

Sunshine Therapy

The entities on the earth plane literally exist under the kind benevolence of the bright, beautiful sun. Alas, our sedentary lifestyle has kept us away from the grace and beneficial rays of the sun, especially the early morning rays. These rays have high healing and restorative properties.

Sunlight kills harmful bacteria and therefore prevents many diseases.

It provides the most essential vitamin D to our body. Vitamin D cannot be found in any source other than sunshine. It is important for the healthy bone function of the body.

Sunshine is known to strengthen muscles, tissues, heart function, circulation and improve metabolism.

A word of caution: do not expose yourself to the hot, glaring afternoon sun especially in a tropical country like India.

Also, allow a lot of fresh air and sunlight into your homes.

Therapy No. 10

Stillness Therapy

Aldous Huxley noted, "The twentieth century is The Age of Noise. Physical noise, mental noise and the noise of desire!"

Silence has extremely high therapeutic value and has been a spiritual tonic from time immemorial. As the health of the mind influences the condition of the body, a calm and still mind is the identity of a fit person.

In this age of noise, it is imperative to make efforts to step out of the daily din and clamour and enter into the Silence within.

The yogis meditating in the caves of the Himalayas lived for an average of 150 years. This only proves that silence is more nutritive to the human psyche than all the health food and supplements in the world.

A Californian doctor states that a mortal can survive a good, healthy life span of over 100 years if he simply practices the right combination of silence, meditation and prayer.

Not only does silence help our spirit and body, it improves mental clarity and cognitive function.

It was St. John of the Cross who said, "Speaking distracts, silence and work collect the thoughts and strengthen the spirit."

In silent prayer and meditation, one can connect with that which is greater than our individual self, our Infinite Source, the Absolute which for want of a better word we call God! When one establishes a link with God, one feels rejuvenated. There is a prevailing sense of positive, calming relaxation. The healing of the body becomes an ongoing automatic process.

Therapy No. 11

Soul Therapy

As we know, the human being is a composite blend of the mind, body and spirit. If man would be truly happy and healthy, it is important that all three are in sync with each other.

The ageless truth of all the scriptures and the Bhagavad Gita is that each one of us is truly the eternal, the deathless spirit. The body is only a garment we wear.

It was Rachel Naomi Remen who observed, "Healing is not a matter of mechanism but the work of the Spirit."

The dynamics of the human body is the soul. It is the hidden spirit, the metaphysical power that is the driving force behind the wonderful workings of all the organs. It is the nourisher of the mind and body.

How Does One Nourish The Spirit?

- By realising that we are the soul and not the physical body. By not getting attached to forms, situations and ideas.

- By practicing the presence of God. With prayer and silence the spirit is strengthened.

- A moment's vital connection with the sublime power of God can bring comfort, grace and all that you seek.

- By constantly reciting the Name of God. The Divine Name has immense healing power. The *rishis* and sages have affirmed repeatedly that the Name Divine is the elixir of life.

Hand over yourself, in loving childlike trust to the Lord. It is important that we become carefree and trusting just like a little child. It is then that no worry, fear or anxiety can ever come close to you!

Therapy No. 12

Laughter Therapy

According to the Doctors and nurses of the American Association For Therapeutic Humour, people often store negative emotions, such as anger, fear, sorrow, instead of expressing them. Laughter helps to release these emotions in a natural and harmless way.

Healers and Philosophers have known about the therapeutic value of laughter for ages. It has only been some time since the value of laughter has been scientifically realised. Today Laughter Clubs, Therapeutic Associations, and laughter groups have come up everywhere.

The benefits of laughter are many: It-

- helps the immune system
- prevents heart disease.
- reduces the incidence of high blood pressure by reducing the release of stress related hormones
- reduces depression, anxiety and psychosomatic disorders. This is because it increases the production of serotonin, a natural antidepressant.
- alleviates pain and fosters a sense of well being by releasing endorphins, the body's pain killer hormones.
  - gives the internal organs of the body a good workout.
  - induces a good and sound sleep.

In the moments of laughter, there is a tendency to remain in the present moment. In this way one forgets the worries of the future and the pain of the past.

When people laugh together, it brings them closer and improves relations. It also helps to enhance communication.

Laughter stimulates both sides of the brain. It helps to keep the person alert and also helps to retain more information.

Practical Ways to Incorporate Humour in our Daily Lives:

- Keep smiling. This is the first step towards laughter. It will keep you on a happy note even if your conditions may not be positive.
- Count your blessings. This is a precursor to the lightness required to truly laugh wholeheartedly.
- Spend time with happy people and those with a sense of humour. Seek the company of people who look at the lighter side of life.
- Spend time with children. They are spontaneous and cherubic all the time. They are the true experts in laughter therapy.
- Take it easy. Nothing in life is worth getting anxious about.
- Learn to laugh at yourself.
- Laugh with others but never at others.

To sum up:

PRACTICAL SUGGESTIONS TO PROMOTE GOOD HEALTH:

1. The foundation of a healthy body is a happy mind. Therefore, let nothing agitate you or disturb your inner peace. Let the motto of your life be:

   Thou knowest everything, Beloved,
   Let Thy Will always be done!
   In joy and sorrow, my Beloved,
   Let Thy Will always be done!

   There is a doctor who says to his patients, "Keep your upstairs (brain) clean and your downstairs (body) will be healthy!"

2. Eat a balanced diet.

3. Drink sufficient water (never alcohol).

4. Take plenty of fresh air and sunshine.

5. Laugh heartily. Laughter is at once a physical, mental and spiritual tonic. If possible, you must laugh heartily three times a day— before taking breakfast, lunch, dinner. But be careful not to laugh at others. Laugh with others and, if you can, laugh at yourself.

6. You must have sufficient sleep.

7. You must have adequate exercise. Walking is the king of exercises.

8. You must have proper elimination (via bowels, kidneys, lungs and skin).

9. Everyday you must spend some time in silence. Pray, meditate, repeat the Name Divine, engage yourself in a loving and intimate conversation with God, do your spiritual thinking.

10. You must adopt a cheerful and positive attitude. And you must always keep away from wrong habits such as smoking, drinking, drugs. Many promising lives have been sacrificed on the altar of wrong habits.

REFLECT AND ACT

Do you know…?

The main determinants of good health:

Biology — the genetic make-up (genes inherited from mother and father). This is a factor we cannot alter.

Lifestyle habits — such as a nutritious low-fat diet; enough exercise; sufficient, sound sleep; avoiding misuse of tobacco, alcohol and other drugs; motor-vehicle and traffic safety; healthy (safer) sexual practices; and stress-reduction. This is something that only we can take care of.

Emotional balance — good self-esteem, feeling "in control" and able to forge intimate relationships. This is one aspect that we have to work on.

Economic and social wellbeing — sufficient income for food and shelter; supportive networks (family, friends, colleagues). This, we must cultivate, to the best extent possible.

A health-promoting environment — i.e. not excessively polluted, clean air and water, adequate sewage disposal. It is our duty to create and protect such an environment, for us and for others.

Access to adequate medical care when needed.

Ask yourself: Am I doing all I can to protect and promote my own health?

IN A LIGHTER VEIN…

Churchill's Eightieth Birthday

One of the photographers present at Winston Churchill's eightieth birthday expressed the hope that he might also photograph the great man on his hundredth birthday twenty years later. "I don't see why not, young man," Churchill replied. "You look reasonably fit to me."

Man's greatest tragedy is – he thinks he has plenty of time!

J.P. Vaswani

TIME MANAGEMENT

Albert Einstein was often asked to explain the general theory of relativity. "Put your hand on a hot stove for a minute, and it seems like an hour," he once declared. "Sit with a pretty girl for an hour, and it seems like a minute. That's relativity!"

WHAT IS TIME MANAGEMENT?

Experts define Time Management as "the art and technique of arranging, organising, scheduling and budgeting one's time for the purpose of generating more effective work and increasing productivity."

Sounds too complicated, doesn't it?

Time Management is not the prerogative of the business and corporate world. Students, teachers, workers, professionals, mothers, you and I – all of us need to understand the value of time and use it effectively.

It was Edison who said, "Time is really the only capital a human being has, and the only thing he can't afford to lose."

In our age of speed and stress, Time is no longer an abstract concept. "Time is money," is the modern *mantra*. In fact, people would argue that time is more precious, more valuable than money!

10 "Lost wealth may be replaced by industry, lost knowledge by study, lost health by temperance, but lost time is gone forever!"

-Samuel Smiles

Time Management is essential for all of us, if we wish:

- To eliminate hurry, hassle, stress and pressure in our daily work and personal life.

- To escape from the clutches of 'deadlines' that threaten to overrun our lives.

- To 'create' time and space in our lives for all that we really want to do.

- To organise our life and work in such a way that we really enjoy 'living' in the fullest sense.

- To fix our goals and set our priorities so that we achieve what matters most to us.

- To escape the clutches of procrastination – that notorious 'thief' of time.

- To give of ourselves, freely and fully, to those who matter the most to us— as also, to our spiritual pursuits, our higher aspirations and creative impulses.

Remember: *Between tomorrow's dreams and yesterday's regrets lies today's opportunity.*

The Lord Siva Nataraja Shrine at Kailash

The Lord Siva Nataraja Shrine site is a wooded hilltop overlooking the Light Of Truth Universal Shrine (LOTUS) and the foothills of the Blue Ridge Mountains. The site is known as Kailash, named after the holy abode of Lord Siva in the Himalayas. Dedicated on 29 March 1991, the shrine houses a seven-foot bronze statue, generously donated by Sri Dr. Karan Singh and his wife Princess Yasho.

Siva, the King of Cosmic Dance, dances within a flaming halo symbolizing the *Pranava* OM. On His right ear is a man's earring and on the left ear is a woman's earring, showing that He is both male and female. The cobras that coil around the hair and body represent the cosmic force of Siva, the Supreme Yogi.

His *Panchakriya*, or five-fold activities, are represented by:

- Hand holding drum = for evolution through sound

- Hand in *Abhaya Mudra* = the "fear not" seal for preservation

- Right leg resting on *Muyalaka* = the subduing of the deluded egoistic soul that has suffered enough and cries for salvation

- Hand pointing to the raised left foot = the grace that saves the soul that cares to come to His Feet

- Hand holding fire = for ultimate dissolution

As long as we remain in ignorance, we go through suffering under His Foot. Then, when we cry for enlightenment, He says, "Fear not. Come unto My Raised Foot and you will be saved.

–Sri Swami Satchidananda

Satchidananda Ashram Yogaville®

Get More Time Out Of Your Life!

Simple steps to make the most of 24 hours

1. Early to bed, early to rise:

Getting up early in the morning is truly a bonus. Not only does it help you to get more work done during the day, but it also sets the *tone* and *pace* of your whole day.

When this early start is invigorated by your personal appointment with God, you will truly find your day transformed!

Start early! Spend your earliest working hours in silent prayer or meditation. Give time to your parents/spouse/children.

Get to work *before* time. Organise your desk. Check your schedule for the day. Hand your day over to God's care – and begin your work.

You will be amazed by what you can achieve!

2. Organise your life in day-tight compartments:

Draw a circle to represent a 24-hour period. Into this circle, chalk out all the work that you think you can achieve, conveniently, comfortably, without stress.

Forget all the rest. It will have to wait for tomorrow.

True, there may be a lot of work that you have to do. But there is a limit to what you can accomplish today. Therefore, put a cap on it!

When the day is over, plan for the next 24 hours.

3. Set your priorities:

Ask yourself what is important for you and your work. Devote time to those activities.

It is very important to eliminate non-essentials from your life – activities which are neither important, nor useful.

4. Don't force yourself to hurry:

"The truly wise ones, are never in a rush to do their work," says the poet, Subrahmanya Bharati. "They work slowly, silently, like the seed that sprouts into life."

Isn't that an amazing image – the seed that sprouts into new life! You cannot put it on *Fast – Forward* mode; nor can you put it in slow motion.

When you hurry, you cannot keep your mind calm and focussed.

Modern lifestyle, culture and work force us to hurry, hurry, all the time! Of course, we need to be quick and efficient in all that we do – but hurry is wasteful!

5. Do one thing at a time:

Don't fritter away your energies attempting to do too many things – chances are, that you will not do justice to any one of them.

- Don't talk on the phone while you are writing a report.

- Don't read while you are eating.

- Don't SMS when someone is talking to you.

- DON'T talk on the cellphone when you are driving! You are jeopardising your life and others' lives!

When you do too many things at a time, the vital power of your mind is scattered, and your mind is distracted, and your work will not be the best that you can do!

HOW YOU CAN OPTIMISE YOUR TIME

- *Reduce clutter! Keep your workspace clean and well laid out.*

Reduce clutter! Clear your mind too, of all the accumulated clutter of negative feelings, needless information and useless thoughts.

Therefore, avoid distractions. You don't have to check your e-mail every fifteen minutes.

- *Learn to delegate.*

You are not indispensable to every task that needs to be done. Trust your colleagues and subordinates: delegate work to them.

- *Identify, plan and review.*

Identify your long-term and short-term goals.

Plan your work – and then work your plan.

Review your activities every day, to see what you have lapsed from your schedule.

INSPIRATION: ACQUIRING DISCIPLINE

A Zen master was teaching his disciple how to develop the right attitude to life and to work.

The disciple asked the master, "How shall I develop mental discipline in my search for truth?"

The master replied, "You must exercise yourself."

"How may I exercise myself?"

"You must eat when you are hungry; you must sleep when you are tired."

"But that is what everyone does. Do you mean to say that is sufficient to exercise oneself to acquire discipline?"

"But that is what most people do not do. When they eat they are doing a hundred things.

"When they sleep they are dreaming of a million things. That is not what I mean by exercise.

Exercise your mind to live in the present moment, whether you are working, eating or sleeping."

Find Time For Life

Once a management teacher wanted to teach his students about the importance of prioritising time.

He brought a big jar with a wide mouth and some materials in a bag.

First he put into the jar about a dozen small rocks. They filled up the jar. He asked the students, "Is there more space?" unanimously the students replied, "No!"

From the bag he removed some loose gravel and poured it into the jar. It filled up the spaces in between. He shook the jar and as it settled to the bottom, he filled some more.

He asked the students again, "Is there room for more?" They replied

in many voices, "Maybe", "It's possible."

The professor poured into the jar some fine sand. He shook the jar and poured some more. He then poured into the jar some water.

He then asked his students, "What do you think is the purpose of this illustration?" One student quickly replied, "No matter how busy your schedule is, if you try very hard you can always fit in more."

The professor shook his head. "The real purpose of this illustration is to understand that if you don't put the big rocks in first then you can never get them in at all."

What do the big rocks signify? They signify time with the family, time with children, prayer and communion with God, spending your time for a worthy cause and helping others whose need is greater than ours.

The professor concluded, "Find time for the Purpose of Life, the rest is all pebbles and sand."

Contributing Time

- If we could all make successful careers, create beautiful families and live in luxury then all of us would be full of joy and bliss all the time. But this is not easy! We all have some challenge or grief staring us in the face.

- The remedy for all of our maladies is to deviate from our own miseries and help others.

- Sadhu Vaswani always said, "All that we are and all that we have is a loan given to us, to be passed on to those whose need is greater than ours."

- Remember nothing belongs to us. Our time, our talents, knowledge, wisdom our possessions and our life itself is a loan given to us.

- People tell me there are so many tasks to be accomplished by us and with so little time, so little energy how can we help? Our resources are limited. Some say, "It's none of our business!" Surely, it's our business. Mankind is our business.

- Those of you who have done so much in life and yet are frustrated, some who feel useless and bored, try the medicine of service: it will bring you great joy. It was Henry Drummond who said, "There is no happiness in having or getting but in giving. Half the world is on the wrong scent in the pursuit of happiness. They think it is in having and getting and being served by others. It consists of giving and serving."

PRACTICAL SUGGESTIONS

Effective Time Management: Software for Success:

The software for success may be spelt out as:

1. Do only that which you feel is right and true. Nothing in life brings about failure more surely than lack of integrity.

2. Do your best each day. Let this be the motto of your life: only the best is good enough for me! When you give to the world the best you have, the best will come back to you.

3. Fully trust in the divine wisdom that designs and orders the scheme of things. There is a meaning of mercy in all that happens.

. Plan for today. Budget your time. The truly successful man fits 26 hours into a day of 24, cutting down waste. Take care of every moment of your time.

Effective Time Management

1. Do you find it difficult to relax □
2. Do you find it impossible to switch off you cellphone? □
3. Do you find it difficult to relax without alchohol or cigarettes? □
4. Do you feel slightly guilty when you are enjoying yourself? □

5. Begin the day right! Wake up, each morning, full of hope and expectation.

6. Never give up! Persistence is the law of success!

7. Tact is better than talent.

8. Stay young all your life! Age is a state of mind.

9. Reach out to others. You succeed in the measure in which you help others to succeed.

REFLECT AND ACT

"Take time to live – because life has so much to give!" proclaims a poster, which depicts a little girl, strolling happily in a beautiful garden, clutching a bunch of flowers.

Do you take time to live – or are you simply filling your time with work?

Take this Quiz to find out the answer:

1. Do you find it difficult to relax – sit still, stare into space, doing nothing?

2. Are you constantly thinking about your work / business even during meals/parties/outings?

3. Do you feel bored and restless on holidays and during vacations?

4. Do you think that working late is a sign of competency and leadership?

5. Do you feel slightly guilty when you are enjoying yourself?

6. Do you find it impossible to switch off you cellphone?

7. Do you devote sufficient time to your life, your leisure and your creative interests?

8. Do you find it difficult to relax without alchohol or cigarettes?

If your answer is *yes* to more than two/three questions, it is time for you to change your working style!

IN A LIGHTER VEIN:

A sales representative, an administration clerk, and their manager are walking to lunch when they find an antique oil lamp. They rub it and a Genie comes out. The Genie says, "I'll give each of you just one wish."

"Me first! Me first!"says the admin clerk. "I want to be in the Bahamas, driving a speedboat, without a care in the world." Puff! She's gone.

"Me next! Me next!" says the sales rep. "I want to be in Hawaii, relaxing on the beach with my personal attendant, an endless supply of Pina Coladas and the love of my life." Puff! He's gone.

"OK, you're up," the Genie says to the manager. The manager says, "I want those two back in the office after lunch."

Lesson: Always let your boss have the first say.

The greatest famine in the world today is the famine of understanding. No two people seem to understand each other today! Therefore, misunderstandings abound in our age. There is misunderstanding in our homes, our clubs, our schools, colleges, universities, corporations and organisations.

I recall the words of the great Parsi Prophet, Zoroaster: "Know well that a hundred temples of wood and stone have not the value of one understanding heart!"

Understanding hearts are what we need, so that people may live and work in harmonious, peaceful co-existence!

J.P. Vaswani

PEOPLE MANAGEMENT

This is a dilemma that was posed before all the applicants to the post of a HR Executive in a reputed company:

You are driving along in your car on a wild, stormy night, it's raining heavily, when suddenly you pass by a bus stop, and you see three people waiting for a bus:

- An old lady who looks as if she is about to die.
- An old friend who once saved your life.
- The perfect partner you have been dreaming about.

Which one would you choose to offer a ride to, knowing very well that there could only be one passenger in your car?

- You could pick up the old lady, because she is going to die, and thus you

should save her first;

- Or you could take the old friend because he once saved your life, and this

would be the perfect chance to pay him back.

- However, you may never be able to find your perfect mate again.

The candidate who was hired had no trouble coming up with his answer. Guess what was his answer?

He simply answered:

"I would give the car keys to my old friend and let him take the lady to the hospital. I would stay behind and wait for the bus with the partner of my dreams."

Sometimes, we gain more if we are able to give up our stubborn thought limitations. We don't necessarily have to be selfish to get the best out of life!

WHAT IS THE SECRET TO ENRICHING HUMAN RELATIONSHIPS?

Are there any special principles that govern these relationships?

How does one understand the nature of all relationships?

We cannot have 'theories' for everything – especially for getting along with people. No blueprint can give us a preplanned design to organise our lives with other people. Human beings are unique, perhaps somewhat illogical, and definitely unprogrammable!

Each one of us is sensitive; each one of us is different; and each one of us is constantly variable—our mood and temperament change from day to day, may be even from hour to hour!

And yet we have evolved into a society, into a community, into a global habitat with families, institutions and corporations.

This has been possible with time, a growing sense of awareness, and a great deal of understanding, tolerance, sympathy and mutual respect.

Every relationship is unique and special.

Parents, spouses, children, family, friends, neighbours, colleagues, superiors, subordinates, employers or employees – every relationship needs to be nurtured with understanding and patience.

The secret of successful relationships is to be found in an understanding heart.

Preferably, your own!

Focus on People's Merits and Strengths

The great Prophet of the Baha'i faith, Baha'u'llah, said to his disciples again and again, "If you find that there are nine vices and only one virtue in your neighbour, forget the nine vices, and focus only on the one virtue."

This is the secret of an understanding heart. See only the good in others.

When we focus on others' faults, we only draw those negative forces unto ourselves.

Fault-finding, constant criticism and magnifying the mistakes of others are poor, ineffective ways of changing the world.

A sunny temperament and a healthy sense of humour can do wonders for you.

Try a smile or a kind word – you will find that wrongs are easy to set right, and 'wrong doers' are set back on the right track!

Inspiration

A young girl called Priya grew so much in the love of God, that she was actually able to commune with Sri Krishna, her *ishta devata*.

A doubting, faithless priest wished to put her to the test. " If, as you claim, you really commune with Sri Krishna everyday, ask Him to tell you what was the sin I committed when I was a young man."

He was sure that she would never find out. And this would expose her claim as being false.

Next week, he sought her out and asked her, "Have you spoken to Sri Krishna?"

"Yes, I did," she replied.

"And did He tell you what was the sin I committed?"

"He told me that He had forgotten it – and wanted you to do the same."

The doubting priest hung his head in shame.

If God does not keep a tally of people's faults and failings, why should we?

Are You Listening?

If you wish to enrich your relationships, learn to be a good listener.

Let the other person talk and prove his point to his satisfaction. Do not interrupt him while he is talking – even if he is your subordinate.

Don't you feel exasperated if someone interrupts what you are trying to say?

"Please let me finish!" are the words uttered most frequently at committee meetings.

Listen more, talk less.

We were made to listen: that is why God has given us two ears and only one mouth.

If we had been given two mouths on either side of our heads and just one ear on our faces, how funny we would look!

Be a good listener; therefore, listen not only with your ears, but with your heart.

Menfolk, especially bosses and husbands, need to work on their listening skills.

Inspiration: Lend Your Ears!

Chandra was a bright and hardworking girl. She had just joined a BPO company. She had no prior work experience. As each day passed she got better and better at her job. But she felt an underlying sense of insecurity. She felt lost in the multitudes of people in the huge company. Being a sensitive person, she felt that she would do better in a smaller company. She thought that she wouldn't mind too much, even if the pay scale was lower.

Chandra felt that she was losing focus and felt a drop in her job satisfaction. After a few days her manager got transferred. The new manager was Ms. Vidya. She was exceptionally warm and congenial.

Whenever Chandra went to knock on her door for a query, Vidya stopped whatever she was doing, and would greet her warmly. She would invite Chandra to sit down, and give undivided attention to what the young lady wished to say. Vidya was always calm, unhurried and totally focused.

This was remarkable for Chandra, because no other manager had ever given her that kind of attention. She felt that she was listened to and that her opinions were important. She suddenly began to feel that her role in the organisation was significant. She changed her mind about leaving the job.

Pure focused listening had helped Vidya to retain the service of a valuable employee.

Appreciate Others

It was William James who said that the deepest need of a human being is the craving to be appreciated.

Praise helps people to reinstate their own self esteem. This, in turn, makes them enthusiastic about what they are doing; they find it worthwhile to achieve targets.

Bonuses, perks and material benefits alone, are not enough to retain people in an organisation and keep them motivated. We need to realise that people's sense of self worth and dignity are high value assets that need to be protected.

For those of us who are always worried about additional expenses, it is good to know that appreciation will make no dents on the pocket, and one can freely use it anytime, anywhere.

A research carried out among young MBA students at a premier institution in India, found that the freshers valued appreciation more than a fat paycheck.

A manpower cosultancy firm found that 58% of the employees they interviewed in a metro city, said that they did not even receive a simple thank-you note for a job that was done well.

Inspiration: Learning To Say Thank You

Deepak Sanghvi sat down to write a letter of thanks to his schoolteacher for having encouraged him so much when he had been in her class thirty years ago. The following week he had received an answer, written in a shaky hand. The letter went like this:

"My dear Deepak, I want you to know what your note meant to me. I am an old woman now, in my seventies. I live in a little room in the outskirts of the town. I live in a lonely abyss that is dragging me deeper everyday. I cook for myself and wonder if I will

make it till the morning. You will be surprised to know that I had taught in school for over forty years and yours is the first letter of appreciation that I have received.

It has brought new hope for me to move on!"

Be A Friend!

A true friend will never come in the way, unless you are on your way down!

How can I be a true friend to the people who matter to me?

- I must permit my friends to be themselves. I must accept them as what they are, for what they are, along with their imperfections.

- I must give my friends their personal space. I must respect their privacy, even as I retain my own.

- I must always be ready to help my friends.

- I must not offer my advice unless it is asked for. And I must offer only constructive advice.

- I must be loyal to my friends – seeing them through good times as well as bad times. We can all do without 'fair weather friends'.

- I must learn to praise my friends and appreciate their achievements.

- I must always be honest with my friends. I must speak out my feelings. I must not bottle up my anger or resentment. For clearing the air will help relationships to grow and flourish. However, I must also bear in mind that some things are best left unsaid.

- I must always trust my friends, and never ever doubt their loyalty or goodness.

> I went out in search of a friend,
>
> I could not find one there!
>
> I went out to be a friend,
>
> And friends were everywhere!

WHO IS A TRUE LEADER?

A leader's qualities are noticed and actually reflected in the organisation he heads.

People subconsciously imitate his traits and in a subtle way his strengths or weaknesses flow throughout the hierarchy of the organisation.

What are the qualities you like to see in the people who work for you?

- Integrity
- Humility
- Honesty
- Openness
- Courtesy
- Charisma
- Credibility
- Trust
- Enthusiasm

Cultivate these qualities yourself – and you will see them mirrored in your people.

Here is a list of simple and cost-effective techniques to boost morale among your employees:

- Learn to express your thanks in words, through official letters and notes.

- Encourage people to come out with their suggestions and opinions. You may not agree with them; but it is good for you to know what they think.

- Share a light moment with them; crack jokes, smile and laugh with them.

- Remember to send them a note or a card on their birthdays.

- Be sensitive to their needs.

- Understand their perspective.

- Encourage creativity and innovation through special awards.

- Make sure that you have realistic expectations of people: remember, each one has different potential.

- Do not try to exercise constant control over people and events. Just give them the right direction.

- Praise deserving staff publicly and at meetings.

CONFLICT MANAGEMENT

Conflicts are not always bad news. Experts tell us that conflicts are necessary to-

1. Raise and address crucial problems.

2. Energise work and focus effort on the most critical issues.

3. Enable people to "be real", to participate, and work together to solve problems.

4. Teach people how to recognise and benefit from their differences.

The conflict is not often the problem - but that the conflict is badly handled, which is the problem.

WHY DO CONFLICTS HAPPEN?

1. Absence of effective organisational communications.

   Employees are not kept informed; they begin to rely on rumours.

2. The allocation of responsibilities is not clearly defined.

   Thus there is disagreement about "who does what".

3. Stress from working with inadequate resources.

   Poor facilities and lack of organisational support cause dissatisfaction among employees.

4. Leadership style becomes a source of conflict, in some cases.

Steps to Minimise Conflicts

1. Ensure that your employees know their roles and responsibilities in the organisation. Get their feedback on the same.

2. Build good relationships with all your subordinates.

3. Get regular, written reports on their activities.

4. Conduct special programmes; plan special retreats to boost their morale.

6. Hold management meetings on a regular basis to communicate new initiatives and discuss the status of current programmes.

7. Consider a suggestion box in which employees can provide suggestions.

PRACTICAL SUGGESTIONS

Here are a few practical suggestions to help you get on well with people — at work, at home, in your extended family and at all levels of your social interactions:

1. Learn to be a good listener – let the other person talk and express his point of view.

2. Do not belittle the other person, do not make him feel small. Do not criticise him or find fault with him.

3. When you find that you cannot get along with others, do not blame them; find the fault in yourself.

4. Remember there can be no true understanding without the spirit of humility.

5. Avoid arguments; when you think you have won an argument, you may have actually lost a friend.

6. Even when you don't argue with people, respect their opinion.

7. Always be on the lookout for opportunities to be of service to others; learn to be sensitive to others' needs.

REFLECT AND ACT

What is your view of the role and responsibilities of a good manager?

Experts tell us of some distinct dimensions of managerial skills, which we do not normally associate with the conventional image of a 'boss'.

1. They are responsible, not only for the productivity, but for the happiness and emotional wellbeing of the people who work under them. (Indirectly and directly, this affects productivity and profits too!)

2. Like the head of a family, or the coach of a sports team, the manager has an emotional responsibility towards his subordinates.

3. It is the manager and his style of functioning that makes the work environment stressful or comfortable; happy or strained; fun or hell!

4. While he has been hired by the organisation to promote its profits, the manager also has a more serious commitment to those who work under him – because their careers, their future are entrusted to his care.

5. It is not merely his job to tell people what to do: it is also his job to encourage people to contribute their ideas and suggestions on all projects undertaken by the company.

6. It is not enough for him to 'keep an eye' on the coming and going and doings of his people: it is also essential for him to give them the freedom and space where they will be able to function at their optimum level.

The best brains and the best talents in an organisation need to be nurtured in an environment that allows them to grow personally and professionally. A good manager keeps them focused, motivated and happy.

What kind of a manager are you?

What kind of a manager would you like to have as your boss?

IN A LIGHTER VEIN:

Motivation and Morale

Once upon a time, a British company and a Japanese company decided to have a competitive boat race on the River Thames. The Japanese won by a mile.

The British firm became very discouraged and morale sagged. Senior Management decided that the reason for the crushing defeat had to be found and a project team was set up to investigate the problem and recommend the appropriate action.

Their conclusion: the Japanese team had eight people rowing and one person steering. The British team had one person rowing and eight people steering.

Senior Management immediately hired a consultant company to do a study of the British team's structure. Millions of pounds and several months later they concluded that too many people were steering and not enough rowing.

To prevent losing to the Japanese next year, the team structure was changed to four 'Steering Managers', three 'Senior Steering Managers' and one 'Executive Steering Manager'. A performance and appraisal system was set up to give the person rowing the boat more incentive to work harder and become a key performer.

The next year the Japanese won by two miles.

You are not the body – you are the immortal spirit within. You are the *atman. Tat twam asi*! That art Thou! Therefore, do not identify with the body, which is just a garment you have worn in this birth.

J.P. Vaswani

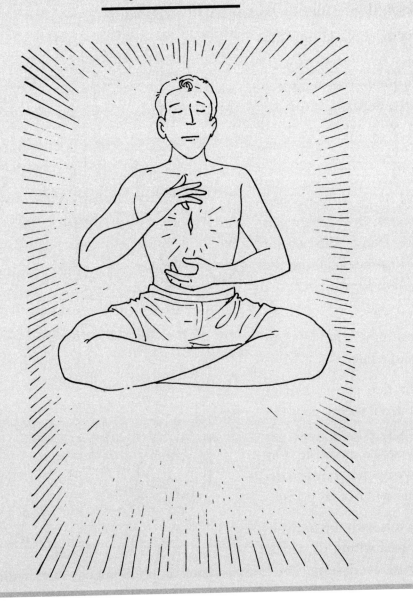

SOUL MANAGEMENT

There was a villager who was invited to visit his rich cousin, who lived in a city. The villager was amazed by the gadgets and electronic marvels that filled his cousin's house. He hit the heights of amazement when he was whisked off to the fifteenth floor office of his cousin, in an elevator.

"This is unbelievable! This is miraculous!" exclaimed the villager. "Truly, cousin, you are great. Why, you have made us go up at the touch of a button!"

As they neared the fourteenth floor, there was a power failure. The elevator came to a standstill, and the lights faded out.

"Can't you do something?" the villager asked in panic.

His rich cousin had to admit that it was actually the electricity which made all the 'marvels' possible. On his own, he could do nothing without its power.

So it is with the body: it is the soul within us which is eternal, everlasting. The body is material, phenomenal, destructible.

WHAT IS THE SOUL?

The soul is the unchanging spirit that pervades all beings. What we call the body, is but a garment that the soul has worn. In the words of the poet Shelley:

> **The One remains: the many change and pass:**
>
> **Heaven's Light forever shines: earth's shadows fly:**
>
> **Life, like a dome of many-coloured glass,**
>
> **Stains the white radiance of Eternity.**

Of the soul, the *atman* within, Sri Krishna says in the Bhagavad Gita:

> **Weapons cleave him not, nor fire burneth him. Waters wet him not, nor wind drieth him away.**
>
> **...He is eternal and all-pervading. He is unchanging and immovable. He is ancient, the same forever...**
>
> **[II 23-24]**

This great reality is difficult for most people to grasp – for so strong, so powerful, so binding is our attachment to the body!

Ancient Indian wisdom likens the soul to a lamp shining within: it is surrounded by three separate sheaths or layers. The mind is the inner layer, the senses constitute the middle layer, and the flesh is the outermost layer.

WHY SHOULD YOU KNOW ABOUT THE SOUL?

When the mind and the senses are unaware of the *atman* within, one becomes egoistical, one allows the ego to dominate one's life and action.

When we are unaware of this great truth – that the soul is eternal, and that the body is mortal – we become obsessed with the physical, material, sensual aspects of life.

People who are obsessed with their physical appearance, suffer from severe stress and insecurity. Each wrinkle, each line on the forehead, each grey hair drives them to distraction.

The more we identify with the body, the more unhappy we become!

Therefore, our *rishis* asserted: *Tat twam asi !*

Therefore, Jesus said to the Jews, "Ye are Gods."

"Your substance is that of God Himself," said a great Sufi saint.

"Whoso knows himself, has Light," said Lao Tse.

If we wish to progress on the path of self-realisation, we *have to* stop identifying ourselves with the body!

Have you ever wondered why pious Hindus remove their shoes before they enter a temple or a holy place? This is merely symbolic of the idea that we move away from our habitual body-consciousness, which will help us move closer to God.

We have got to move away from the body, even as we move away from the "shoes" we wear!

DISCOVER THE STILL CENTRE WITHIN!

Psychologists tell us that there are three 'states' in which human beings exist: the waking state, the sleeping state and the dreaming state.

But Western Psychology stops just a little short of what our ancient sages tell us: a *fourth* state of intense concentration beyond these three – a state of which most of us are unaware!

We are content to live our lives on the surface. Superficiality characterises everything we do. We occupy our minds with what we would like to eat, what we would like to buy, and what we could do to impress our friends and neighbours.

We have no time to think of the world within!

Within us, lies a centre of tranquility, serenity, self-knowledge and true awareness. When we touch this still centre within, we will experience true freedom – freedom from the fears, desires, tensions, insecurities and complexes that haunt us in our worldly life.

Therefore, does our Indian tradition place great value on meditation, reflection and contemplation – on that state of inner silence and inner stillness.

It is within us, that we will find the peace and joy we seek so desperately!

In this state, too, we will experience true freedom – freedom from fears, desires and negative thoughts.

In this state, we will discover our own Divinity – that we are not the pathetic, helpless creatures we take ourselves to be, but the eternal, infinite spirit of pure, true, everlasting bliss – *sat chit ananda.*

WHY MEDITATION?

Meditation is the art of quietening, calming the mind, so that our inner consciousness is stilled, and we become deeply aware.

There are several reasons why meditation is essential to all of us:

- The unbearable stress and strain of modern life needs to be countered with conscious stress reduction techniques. Meditation is the most effective among them.

- Meditation unclutters the mind, empties it of negative thoughts and energises the nervous system.

- It strengthens our creativity, our problem-solving skills and our inner sense of harmony.

- It enhances our powers of love, compassion, forgiveness and understanding, making us better human beings.

- It increases what the Zen Masters call "mindfulness" – awareness of the present moment, that enables us to get the best out of our life, every moment.

- It is the best known antidote to restlessness and fragmented thinking.

- It improves our concentration, focus and memory.

STEPS TO CULTIVATE SOUL MANAGEMENT

1. Practise Silence Everyday!

We live in a world of deafening noises. Particles of noise cling to our souls: our souls need to be washed in the waters of silence.

Silence cleanses. Silence heals. Silence strengthens. Silence reveals!

Silence leads you to discover the greatest truth of your life – it teaches you who you really are!

Practise silence everyday, preferably at the same time and at the same place – for this is our daily appointment with our true self.

Begin with just fifteen minutes of silence, then gradually increase the period to at least one hour. Soon you will realise that practising silence is the most worthwhile activity of the day!

2. Become Aware Of The Breath

Prana or breath is the primary energy of life. It is this which links the body with the mind. Hence its importance to our mental, physical and spiritual well-being.

Pranayama is a unique, systematic deep-breathing exercise, associated with yoga and meditation. When it is practised properly, it enables the lungs to absorb optimum levels of oxygen so as to purify the blood, and ease the strain on the heart.

Deep breathing brings immense benefits to us, including a stable mind, steady thinking, inner peace, good health and a longer life.

3. Discover The Value of Mantras

Naam smaran, mantra japa – chanting and repetition of the Name Divine – are the very foundation of *abhyasa*. Together, they quieten the agitated mind, cleanse the mind of all its impurities, leaving us calm and serene.

Concentrate on a *mantra*, a Holy Name, a Word or Syllable, which is close to your heart, and symbolic of the Divine. Repeat it again and again. Repeat it with deep love and longing of your heart. Repeat it until it gets fixed in your mind and is secured in the depths of your consciousness all the time – whether you are working or asleep.

4. Realise that Meditation is for all of us

Many people labour under the erroneous notion that meditation is meant only for ascetics, renunciates and "unworldly souls".

On the contrary, meditation is beneficial to all people of all ages. The negative forces of modern living can be neutralised through meditation.

The curative powers and energies within us can be harnessed through meditation practises and used effectively to fight mental and physical ailments.

5. Cultivate the Spirit of Service

If there is one thing we all seek, it is inner peace.

Peace cannot be achieved by politics, power and diplomacy. True peace is possible only through the spirit of service.

If I had a million tongues, I would appeal to you with each one of them, especially to my young friends who are going to be tomorrow's leaders and pinion makers: Seek not power! Seek service!

Let us do as much good as we can, to as many as we can, in as many ways as we can.

Can you read? Then read to a blind student. Can you write? Then write a letter, fill a form for someone who is not so lucky. If you are not hungry — share your food with someone who is. If you are happy, contended, at peace with yourself – reach out to those who are not as fortunate as you.

We all have something to give! Let us give with love and compassion, and we will make the world a better place, and make ourselves better human beings!

How can I refrain from quoting those beautiful lines that have never failed to inspire me!

> I shall pass through this life but once.
>
> Any good, therefore, that I can do
>
> Or any kindness that I can show to any fellow creature,
>
> Let me do it now.
>
> Let me not defer or neglect it,
>
> For I shall not pass this way again.

6. Learn the value of Acceptance

Nothing, nothing ever happens in our lives without the sanction of Providence.

The really wise ones know that everything happens according to the Will of God.

And in God's Will is our true peace.

Many things happen to us, which, with our puny intellect, we cannot fully understand. Therefore, learn to trust in the Will of the Lord.

To accept the Will of God is to know that all that happens, happens for the best.

The more we grow in this realisation, the happier and more peaceful shall we feel. Cultivating the spirit of acceptance brings us true security and lasting peace.

SEEK A SPIRITUAL MENTOR

In an age of Self-Help Books, Self-Improvement Practices and Do-It-Yourself Ideas, it is not surprising that people should raise the question: Why do we need a Guru? Is not self-realisation possible with individual effort? Can we not seek liberation for ourselves?

Why do we need the Guru? The Guru is the great cleanser, a great purifier – not merely a great teacher.

How many of you will keep your child at home, and decide that you will educate him yourselves? You will do no such thing. You will seek out the best schools in your vicinity; some of you might even choose a Residential school far away from home so that he may receive the best education possible. Are you not entrusting your child to the care of good teachers?

Today, cooking is considered as both an art and science, and is taught in a special programme to aspiring chefs, in institutions of catering technology. A cook needs the guidance of cooking experts to teach him the intricacies of food preparation, presentation and aspects of nutrition.

We have driving schools all over the place, where trained instructors will teach you how to drive a car.

We have colleges of arts and fine arts where aspiring painters, sculptors and artists are trained to express their creativity in the best possible manner.

The 'lesson' is obvious. We need the guidance of an expert to acquire mastery over any subject. We must be willing to devote our time, attention and effort to acquire knowledge / wisdom / skill from him – or else, we would remain ignorant.

What about the life of the spirit? If we take so much trouble over worldly education, must we not devote even greater care and effort to equip ourselves for our journey on the spiritual path?

The Guru is not only your guide and guardian on the spiritual path – he is also a great facilitator who helps you achieve inner progress.

If you concede that such expert authority is essential to your physical well-being, would you still like to treat your spiritual well-being, on a lower plane, treating it as a Do-it-yourself matter?

REFLECT AND ACT:

Here is a simple technique in five steps to cultivate the soul:

- Always entertain positive thoughts. Never harbour thoughts of jealousy, hatred, greed or envy.

- Do not react emotionally, rashly to things that happen.

- Never give in to making negative suggestions about yourself. Don't say, "I can't cope," "I can't handle this," or "I have a bad memory." Always think positive thoughts about yourself.

- Never hate or resent people. Let love and forgiveness be the law of your life. Intense hatred and resentment can lead to many types of illnesses.

- Read books that inspire and uplift you. Avoid books that feature violence, sex, crime and vice.

To Sum Up:

Practical Suggestions on How To Meditate:

- Sit in Silence. Sit comfortably but with the spine, neck and head aligned.

- Practice meditation preferably at the same time and at the same place.

- Face the East or the North.

- Go to the Infinite Source as you are, with your faults and failings.

- Think of an object or a symbol, a teaching, a name or incident from the life of a great one.

- As you sit in silence let your face wear a gentle smile.

- Repeat a *mantra*. *Mantras* are a combination of powerful sacred words which reflect their divine attributes on the person chanting.

- Visualise every part of your body becoming a source of light and love.

- Visualise yourself as a spark of the bright infinite luminosity that lights up this entire universe.

In A Lighter Vein:

Mullah Nasruddin would sit everyday for eight hours, in silence, with his ear against a wall. He did this day after day. One day, his wife asked him, "Mullah, you sit with your ear stuck to the wall everyday. Tell me, what do you hear?" The Mullah replied, "If you wish to hear, you must come and sit here yourself." Next morning, the wife got up very early and prepared the day's meals quickly, so that she would be free to go and sit all day with her ear against the wall. She sat for four long hours– but she heard nothing. Exasperated, she said to the Mullah, "I have sat here for four hours and I have heard nothing. I am tired and I am giving up now." The Mullah retorted, "You want to give up after four hours. I have been sitting thus for eight hours everyday for the last 28 years, I have not heard anything either. But I do not give up!"

AFTERWORD

The gift of life has been bestowed on all of us, that we may find fulfillment and grow in perfection.

Life is wonderful! If you feel that your life is not wonderful, and needs to be changed for the better, you must cultivate the soul! Joy, love, purity, peace, prayer, contentment, acceptance and the selfless spirit of service must permeate your spirit; then you will find that your world will change, and your whole environment will shape itself in accordance with your persistent thinking.

Therefore, let us make our lives truly wonderful! Let us:

1. Realise what we are in essence.

2. Count our blessings.

3. Become "thank you" people, cultivating the spirit of gratitude to God.

4. Keep the gate closed on the past.

5. Make today count.

6. Trust in the goodness and caring power of God.

7. Let go, let go, let God!

May the Grace of God and the Guru make your endeavour successful!

NOTES

NOTES